Clearing the Air One Nose at a Time

CARING FOR YOUR PERSONAL FILTER

by
Hana R. Solomon, M.D.

This book is not intended to replace or interfere with your doctor's recommendations or substitute for medical advice, and you should consult with your health care professional for matters relating to your health. This book is intended to share information and offer suggestions for improved and informed health care choices.

Book cover designed by Hana R. Solomon, M.D.

All drawings, images, and tables were created by Hana R. Solomon, M.D., except for the following:

- History of nasal wash devices, original drawings obtained from United States Patent and Trademark Office records.
- Photo of Mechanical Sinus Irrigator, from GOOGLE images.
- Photo of Sophie Murphy, from KOMU-TV.
- Photo of Rachel and Matthew Griffith, by Michael Griffith.
- Copy of Dr. Sage's Nasal Douche sketch, from "The People's Common Sense Medical Advisor" by R.V. Pierce, M.D.

Special heartfelt gratitude to Stacey M. Kerr, M.D.
Helped me roof the barn 36 years ago,
Canned salsa and picked green beans while listening to my complaints,
Gazed at the stars in the hot tub and edited my written thoughts.
Thank you my dear friend.

Cataloging-in-Publication information available from the Library of Congress
ISBN: 978-1-60743-623-2

$15.00
ISBN 978-1-60743-623-2
51500>

9 781607 436232

8 90668 00007 4

"Being a family physician with chronic allergies, vasomotor rhinitis, and sinus issues, I know the nose inside and out. I know how great an effect the nose has on our overall health and sense of well being. I am so grateful for Dr. Hana's book because it explains the anatomy, function, and care of the nose in easy to understand terms that I can share with my patients. In my practice I stress patient empowerment and preventive medicine, and I plan to enthusiastically recommend her well written and complete book to anyone with a nose!"

Stacey Kerr M.D., Board Certified Family Physician and
author of *Homebirth in the Hospital*

"Nasal saline irrigation is a simple, scientifically proven method for preventing and treating so many respiratory health problems. It has been a breakthrough for my patients with recurrent sinus infections, nasal congestion, asthma and colds. Every day I teach people to incorporate this time-honored and effective technique into their daily health program. Clearing the Air, One Nose at a Time *is a must-read for every doctor who sees patients and every patient with a nose!*"

Jane Murray, M.D., Board Certified in Family Medicine and Holistic Medicine
Medical Director, Sastun Center of Integrative Health Care, Overland Park, KS

"In an easy to understand fashion, Dr. Hana's book clearly outlines many of the concepts involved with the care of the ears, nose and throat. This book places Dr. Hana as the expert in the science of nasal washing, and it should be required reading for anyone with nasal and sinus problems. It is time that nasal washing be used as a front line treatment for nasal and sinus complaints as well as for prevention."

Kelvin Walls, M.D., Board Certified Ears, Nose and Throat Specialist and
American Academy of Otolaryngology-Head & Neck Surgery Member

"I have been using a nose washing system for two years and I swear by it and after reading Dr. Solomon's book I now know why it works."

Bill Wax, Program Director and show host of
Sirius/XM Satellite Radio's B.B. King's Bluesville

Dedication

This book is dedicated to those who will never be able to read this book, yet these words and ideas belong to them.

To all those who taught me and all who held my hand.

To my late grandmother Sabta, who demonstrated how to really survive. She survived the Holocaust with 4 children all intact and taught me to be strong no matter what the obstacles.

To my mother, Elza Drapacz, whose wisdom, compassion and never-ending faith in me allowed me to be free to find me. She taught me how to be appreciative of what I did have. (If I came home with a cut on my eye, she would say, "Thank God it wasn't both eyes.")

To my children, Josh, Vera, Rachel, and Marcus who accept my still-youthful dreams and who are each living their own dreams.

To my late sister Jeannie, who showed me how to taste all the spices that life offers, who danced to her own music and who helped me grow up.

To my late father who showed me the value of spirit, guts, artistic expressions and how to have fun.

To my late grandfather Sabba, Marcus Drapacz, who demonstrated to me the value of accepting others and who, in his 80's, speaking no English and barely able to get around, traveled from the East Coast to the middle of Missouri just so he could share my communal family experience on The Farm. No judgment, just acceptance and love of nature.

To my lifelong best friend and endless supporter, no matter how outlandish my current dream may be, my husband George.

This book is dedicated to all those who struggle with their nose and to those I hope will learn to appreciate that wonderful filter.

Hana R. Solomon, M.D.
Columbia, Missouri

Table of Contents

Introduction 1-4
How To Use This Book 5
Master Diagrams 6, 7

Part I
Chapter 1   **Lay Of The Land — Overview Of The Nose** 9, 10
Primary Function Of The Nose: Defend, Protect,
And Shield. 11, 12
The Magic Of Mucus 12, 13
Mucus And Its Many Colors: Help! My Mucus Is Green! 14
The Cilia Sweep 15
Smell and Taste. 16
Moods 17
Sexuality 17
Other Uses For Your Nose. 18
Sinuses — What Are They And Why Do We Have Them? . . . 18-22
As The Nose Goes, The Ears Follow 22-25
The Eyes Have It — An Intimate Connection With The Nose . . . 25

Chapter 2   **Paying Through The Nose — The Cost Of Nasal Woes** . . .27-29

Chapter 3   **Medications** 31
Medications & Additives For The Nose:
Used, Misused, Abused 31
Nasal Medications, Preservatives & Additives 31
Nasal Spray Addiction: *Rhinitis Medicamentosa* 32
Decongestants. 33
Antihistamines 34
Other Medications 35-37

Part II
Chapter 4   **Nasal Washing —**
Dilution Is The Solution To The Pollution 39
Why Has Nasal Washing Become So Popular? 39

Why Do Medical Providers Need To Know
About Nasal Washing?. 40
The History Of Nasal Irrigation 40-42
The Evolution Of Nose Washing Devices. 43

Chapter 5   Ins & Outs Of Nasal Washing —
Taking Care Of Your Great Defender 45
Why Wash Daily?. 45
Who Should Wash?. 46, 47
Who Should *Not* Wash?. 48
When To Wash? 48
How Frequently To Wash?. 49
What To Wash With? 49
Solutions And Salt Facts You Should Know 51
Hypertonic 52-55
Isotonic 56
Hypotonic. 57
Buffering, pH And Acidity 57, 58
Additives For Your Nose Wash Solution?. 61-63
Nose Wash Style — So Many Choices! How To Choose? 63
The Importance Of Head Position 63-65
Consider The Volume 65
Technique And Style 66
For Moderate To Severe Congestion. 66
A Comfortable Habit. 67
All In One Place: Common Nose Washing Systems 68-73

Chapter 6   Nasopure 75
The Nasopure Effect. 76-80
Detailed Instructions For Using The Nasopure System 81
Possible Side Effects Of Nasal Washing 84

Part III
Chapter 7   Children 93
Kids And Colds — The Seemingly Endless Connection 93
Children And Ears 94-98
School Days 98, 99
Teaching Your Child To Wash. 100
What If Your Preschool Child Is Scared Of Water? 101

How To Teach Your 2-3 Year Old Toddler To Wash. 102-104

How To Teach Your 4-6 Year Old To Wash 105

How To Teach Your 7-9 Year Old To Wash. 106

How To Teach Your Child To Blow His Or Her Nose 107

Chapter 8 Just For Women. 113

Pregnancy And Hormones 113

Woman And Heart Disease: Is Air Pollution A Factor?. 114

Chapter 9 The Seasoned Schnozz. 117

Chapter 10 When Your Defense Is Down 123

Viral Infections 123

The Common Cold vs. That Dreaded Flu Virus 123

The Common Cold. 125-128

Reminders When You Have A Cold. 128-133

Sinus Problems And Bacterial Infections 133

Chronic Sinusitis 133-139

Fungal Sinusitis 139

Allergies And Hay Fever 141-147

Sore Throats: 'My Throat Is Killing Me!' 147-149

The Scoop On Strep 149, 150

Post-Nasal Drip 151

Constant Runny Nose *(Vasomotor Rhinitis)* 151-152

Cough, Cough, Cough. 152-156

Asthma: Inflammation Of The Airways. 156-160

Sleep And Breathing Problems —

More Serious Than You May Think 160-162

Vocal Cord Dysfunction 162

Ears And Hearing Problems 163

Eustachian Tube Dysfunction (ETD). 164

Outer Ear Infection — Swimmers Ear. 164

Middle Ear Infection *(Otitis Media)*. 164, 165

Bad Breath *(Halitosis)* 165, 166

Nose Bleeds *(Epistaxis)* 166-169

Nasal Polyps. 169, 170

Deviated Nasal Septum. 170-172

Decreased Or Absence Of Smell *(Anosmia)*. 172

Immotile Cilia. 173

Cystic Fibrosis 174, 175

Resistant Bacteria 175, 176

Chapter 11 Normal Life Needs 177

Can't I Just Buy An Air Filter 177, 178

Professional Voices. 178-180

Military. 180

Travelers 181, 182

Smokers. 182

What's That Smog In The Air 183-185

Living & Working In Polluted Environments. 185-187

Athletes & Sports Enthusiasts. 187

Bicycles & Motorcycles 188, 189

Golfers. 189

Hikers, Campers & Gardeners 190

Scuba Divers. 190

Conclusion 193, 194

References 195-197

Introduction

Let's talk about your nose.

Let's talk about your kids' noses and your partner's nose and your grandparents' noses and your friends' noses...

In fact, let's talk about *everyone's* nose, because I know noses and what I know can help you.

Why do I care so much about the nose? Why should you care?

The nose is more than just a bump in the middle of your face or a place for your sunglasses to rest. It is a part of your body that communicates with your outer world. It allows babies to continuously suckle on their mother's breast while easily breathing. The nose has the power to change your entire consciousness and mood in a single second — just expose your nose to a skunk. Or better yet, take a whiff of a rose.

The nose is our gatekeeper, our personal filter and our great defender.

And when a nose fails in some fashion, it affects the ears, sinuses, throat, appetite and disposition. A dysfunctional nose can cause headaches, snoring, coughing, and asthma; the list goes on and on.

I know noses. Trust me, I'm a doctor. Shucks, as a pediatrician for over 20 years, I consulted with innumerable patients whose noses were snotty, congested, itchy, drippy, plugged, dry, sneezy, bloody and overmedicated. My common sense first response has always been, "WASH IT first."

It all began with my mother and my Sabta, back in Brooklyn during the 1950s. My grandmother always insisted on chicken soup for any illness. Despite her petite stature, she would declare, in her native tongue: "Eat. It's good for you!" On the other hand, I'm certain I never heard Sabta say, "Take this medicine. It'll make you better." As a child, I do not recall ever being given a pill for anything, *ever*. Only once did my doctor insist on a medication, a shot no less, when I was really ill. I guess you could say I was raised to have an "arms-length" relationship with the medical community.

During the 70s, in my early twenties, I joined a group whose lofty goal was to change the world by living off the Earth and leaving a tiny carbon footprint. There I found inner peace by growing organic food and preserving as much as possible for those long cold winters out on The Farm. I centered my life on beans, greens, meditation and forgiveness. In this way, I was hoping to repair and change the world.

But the world was not changing fast enough and we were dirt poor. I could barely help myself, let alone anyone else. My teenage experience of volunteering as a Candy Striper in a Brooklyn hospital seeded my idea of being a doctor, but I lacked confidence. I had no role models to encourage me to pursue this outlandish notion. Me? A doctor? You must be joking! But somewhere, in the deepest part of me, against everything in my history to that point, I still wanted to be a doctor.

I dared not voice my dream. That is, until my personal growth experience of living on the Earth with beans, greens and meditation fertilized my determination and strength.

So when I was twenty-seven I left The Farm and began undergraduate college with the goal of becoming a doctor. I completed four years of college in three years, and exactly three years after my exit off The Farm, I started my first day of medical school as a single mom with two children.

The women in my family demonstrated for me, through their own lives, how to live as independent thinkers. My learning process was most certainly skewed by my life experiences, maturity, and appreciation for the natural world. I was primarily interested in prevention and avoiding invasive medications and surgeries. I listened intently when professors taught me compassion and patient empowerment. The technical skills of surgical procedures, the nuances of x-ray procedures, and the minutia of medical regulations were things I grasped quickly, and while I understood their importance, I found them tedious. More importantly, I knew through my own life experiences that the body is a miraculous organism, often able to heal itself if supported in the right environment.

Throughout medical school and residency, I was blessed to receive training from a spectacular teacher of healing. As I listened to his lectures, I did not know the extent of his rare gift, but I did appreciate that he was special. Dr. Gullio Barbero, a pediatric gastroenterologist, would often take four hours or more to hear a family's story. *Really, four hours.* He taught all of us, both the medical students and the residents, that you must start at the beginning: the childhood of the parents. Then you must follow that timeline all the way to the current tummy ache; so four hours was actually the *abridged* version. He demonstrated how this was the first step to understanding the way to heal compassionately. You must listen. The rest is easy.

Another remarkable teacher was Dr. David Parsons, an ear, nose and throat surgeon. His general message was, in essence, "First, do no harm." This is, of course, part of the Hippocratic Oath, which all doctors take upon graduating from medical school. Dr. Parsons' specialties were sinus surgery, ear tube placements, tonsillectomies, and adenoidectomies. However, his message was, "Never perform surgery on a child if it can be avoided." He shared the notion that irrigation of the nose makes sense *before* a patient goes into the operating room. He taught that washing could even *prevent* a trip to the operating room.

I took this advice to heart.

During the decades since completing my medical training, I have learned much about the nose. For years I shared a clinic with my husband who is a family physician, so I have seen my share of adult issues in the nose, sinus, ears and lungs. Let's face it: I developed into the "snotty nose" expert. I studied, reviewed, discussed and listened to my patients and found I often encouraged nose washing as a way to avoid or reduce the need for medications. I also reviewed published scientific literature regarding nasal irrigation, and I found enormous support for this simple idea. More importantly, I asked every one of my patients to tell me about their experiences with nasal washing. Then I compared this feedback with the formal studies published in the medical literature.

On the other hand, for over 15 years, the majority of my colleagues just didn't get it. They were not incorporating nasal washing into their practices.

My patients confirmed what I witnessed to be true: those who washed their nose daily came to see me less often. Those who washed daily used fewer medications. Those who washed saved lots of money. Those who washed slept better, snored less, and experienced fewer asthma episodes.

A long time ago, we learned that if we brush our teeth daily, we prevent cavities. So now we brush. We know that all sorts of filters, whether for the car, the clothes dryer, the home heating and cooling system … all work better if kept clean. Why not clean the body's filter?

This makes sense to me. In addition, it has made sense to Buddhist monks for millennia. Jala Neti is the ancient practice of nasal washing performed as a daily hygiene routine in the eastern world. Even our grandmothers knew that moisture in the nose makes sense. Have you ever sniffed salt water when you had a cold? Remember placing your head over a steamy pot or in the warm shower when you were ill? Ever used a humidifier? How about that clean feeling after an ocean swim? Washing the nose uses a similar principle, but *far more easily, efficiently and effectively.*

So the question for me was, why did so many patients NOT follow my simple suggestion? Every parent knows that when a child falls and scrapes a knee, the wound is first washed and *then* an antibiotic ointment is applied, if necessary. So, what was preventing more of my patients from incorporating nasal cleansing as a daily hygiene practice?

There were many hurdles. Convenience was a great big hurdle. Availability was a hurdle. The "yuck" factor was a common obstacle. "You want me to do what?" "And where?!" was a familiar response from patients. Therefore, I began my journey of finding the ideal nose washing system for my patients.

I am a medical doctor who thinks like a mom. I have been teaching nasal washing since long before it was "cool." I was "green" before that was cool, too. I have witnessed, both as a patient and as a physician, the value and effectiveness of a preventive, holistic, patient empowerment approach. As a pediatrician, I have seen thousands of snotty noses, ear infections, sinus issues and asthma episodes. And my focus has been on avoidance of medications whenever possible. First, 'Do No Harm.'

This book is not intended to be a comprehensive compilation of all the issues related to the nose, nor a medical reference book. It is, however, full of good information and common sense knowledge which I believe might be helpful in your journey to learn more about your body's air filter and how it relates to your overall health.

In life, as in medicine, nothing is absolute; everything is relative. The more you know, the better able you are to make choices that fit into your personal belief system, your experiences, and your preferences. I share this with you so you can become more empowered.

And one more thing, and let's get this straight: We are talking about snot, goobers, boogers and mucus here so please do not be offended.

How To Use This Book

This book is for you if...

You have a nose,

You are the parent of sick and snotty-nosed kids,

You are a health care provider,

You live or work in a polluted environment, or

You want to have fewer ailments that begin in the nose, use less medication and visit the doctor less often.

Part I is an overview for everyone who has a nose. You will find detailed, scientific explanations of the anatomy, functions and dysfunctions of the nose and related organs in this section. I feel it's important that you become familiar with the basics. Remember, the more you know, the better equipped you are to make decisions.

Part II is about how to clean your nose and how to keep this important filter working well for you.

Part III covers specific conditions for various groups of people. Choose the sections that apply to you.

You will find the Master Diagrams helpful as a point of reference, as you read this book.

Full disclosure: This book is a plea, a pitch, an argument, an appeal, even a nag in favor of daily nose washing. It is not an endorsement for Nasopure, a product that I have developed and patented. I have intentionally removed most references to my system except in the specific chapter entitled Nasopure. However, I want to be clear: I can't discuss and present the most up-to-date comprehensive information on nasal washing without mentioning Nasopure. So I hope that my full and complete disclosure here "clears the air" and explains any perceived product endorsement you might find in this book.

What is far more important is this: Daily washing will keep your nasal passages and sinuses clean, clear and healthy. Allergists, family doctors, pediatricians, ear, nose and throat surgeons, naturopathic physicians and nurse practitioners all agree that nasal washing is safe and effective. You will hear from many of these experts as you read this book. What might be even more meaningful is that tens of thousands of people agree that nose washing, done correctly, feels good and refreshing and actually improves the quality of their lives. I truly don't care what you use to wash as long as *you use something every day to keep your nose clean and healthy.*

Welcome to our knowledge place.

Master Diagram

1 - Maxillary Sinus
2 - Frontal Sinus
3 - Turbinates
4 - Sinus Drainage - Ostiomeatal
    Complex (OMC)

5 - Eustachian Tube
6 - Ear Drum
7 - Sphenoid Sinus
8 - Eustachian Tube Opening
9 - Tonsils

Master Diagram

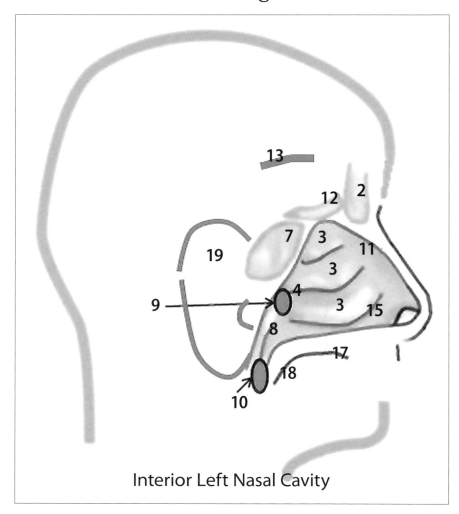

Interior Left Nasal Cavity

10 - Adenoids	15 - Tear Drainage
11 - Blood Vessels	16 - Septum
12 - Olfactory Nerves	17 - Hard Palate
13 - Eyebrow	18 - Soft Palate
14 - Tear Duct	19 - Ear

CHAPTER 1

Lay Of The Land — Overview Of The Nose

 I have always practiced medicine with a basic premise: My patients and I are a team. I listen to their values, preferences, and experiences so that I can understand their needs. I then share what I know, both book and clinical knowledge. People will ultimately make their best choice; being an informed consumer makes the most sense for ideal health. With this in mind, I'd like to share my knowledge of the nose and all related structures so you can choose what works for you. This book is not intended to be comprehensive, but will be thorough as it relates to nasal health. All the scientific minutia one wishes to learn can be found in other publications and in references listed in this book.

The nose is an elegant structure, beautifully designed for essential and life supporting functions. It is not simply an air intake port. When the nose works well, it filters, warms and humidifies the air we breathe — no small task in today's environment. The nose is the first major defense the human body has to protect us from our polluted world. For example, a sneeze is the body's initial protection to expel something considered noxious or even dangerous.

Without this filtering mechanism, millions of impurities would be allowed into our fragile lung tissues, wreaking havoc and damaging the gas exchanging membranes deep within our chests. Without the oxygen humidifying mechanism in our nose, our throat and airways would be dry and irritated all the time, and our moist lungs would dry out like a sponge left in the sun.

What we see of the nose is simply its outer covering and the two intake portals. The outer shape creates the illusion that the nose goes *up*. However, the nose really goes straight back into your head. The medical providers who specialize in the nose can safely insert a probe into your nose, directed straight back without any discomfort yet a probe cannot be inserted upward more than a fraction of an inch. This common misconception has implications you will learn about as you read on. Remember, the nasal passages tunnel straight back!

Even when we are forced to breathe through our mouths, our bodies attempt to moisturize the incoming air by using the tongue as a makeshift humidifier. The healthy and clear nose is a much more efficient and effective air conditioner than the tongue. The nose needs to expose a maximum amount of its intake to the air conditioning apparatus, so it is divided into two wind tunnels (*nostrils*) separated by a thin layer of cartilage called the *septum*.

Septum

The nose is completely divided into two chambers (nostrils) by the septum. At the end of the septum, the single chamber is called the *nasopharynx*. Each nostril is designed to increase surface area with three rolls of tissue *(turbinates)* on each side. The air we inhale passes over these turbinates, picking up moisture along the way.

Turbinates

As the air swirls and spins, it passes across tiny hairs built into the lining of the nose. The filtering system is the sticky mucus in two layers, which act much like a magnet. This mucus is then moved out or swept clean by the cilia. Each is vital to the cleansing of the nose and each cannot function without the other. Together, they capture particles before they can reach the tender lungs and cause damage. Hairs just inside the nostril are course, but the ones further back are small and microscopic. When allowed to move freely and not gummed up by debris and mucus, these tiny hairs *(cilia)* do an excellent job of cleaning the air we breathe and protecting our lungs.

Sometimes an irritant gets caught, either on those folds of tissues called turbinates or in the cilia. When this happens, we might sneeze or our nose may itch. More mucus is produced and our nose lining swells, resulting in the familiar congested feeling. All of these reactions are really part of the body's design to protect itself from impurities. We can help the nose filter more effectively by washing this air conditioning system. Flushing the filter clean is an effective way to help our nose do its job in today's complex and sometimes unclean environment.

Primary Function Of The Nose:
Defend, Protect And Shield

There are many nasal irritants in our world: smoke (fires and cigarettes), allergens, pollution, infectious particles (virus, bacteria, fungus) and excessive mucus. Amazing things happen immediately after one is exposed to irritants.

First, those rolls of tissues (*turbinates*) swell. Increased mucus production occurs. The mucus gets thicker and stickier. The filtering hairs (*cilia*) become clogged. As a result, all the normal drainage systems fail to function. Excessive mucus drips down the throat. There is a decrease in our ability to smell, taste, or hear. We may notice increased sinus pressure, headaches, bad breath or decreased exercise tolerance. Symptoms of chronically obstructed drainage include fatigue, poor appetite, decreased ability to concentrate and even bloody noses.

Irritants are not the only cause of nasal congestion. Air that is cold or dry can also cause congestion of your nasal passages. The congestion slows the airflow to ensure that your lungs receive warm and moist air. And while this reaction may help protect your lungs, the resulting congestion is not pleasant.

The nasal opening, with its general rounded shape, follows basic laws of physics. Any decrease in the radius decreases the actual amount of airflow enormously. In practical terms, a tiny amount of swelling in the nasal passages can result in significant discomfort.

Turbinates

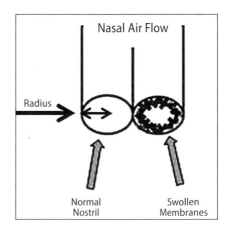

Nasal Air Flow

Radius

Normal Nostril

Swollen Membranes

The turbinates' tissue folds increase surface area so more of the inhaled air can be conditioned. But what else is in the nose that allows it to act as such a great defender against irritants? Let's look at *mucus* and *cilia*.

The Magic Of Mucus

Secreted by special cells, mucus is the substance that you know as "snot," "boogers," or "goobers" — terms that our children delight in saying. Nasal discharge, nasal drainage, rhinitis, and exudates are also terms used to describe this stuff.

But let's clear up the difference between *mucus* and *mucous*. Mucus is the stuff we know as nasal discharge. Mucous is the actual lining of the nose and the sinuses.

Mucous membranes blanket the nose and other body parts. This membrane lining contains special *goblet cells* that produce mucus, a complex substance that keeps the nose and sinuses moist. We produce between 1 pint and 1 quart of mucus per day, thanks to goblet cells. That's 2-4 cups or 8-16 ounces per day!

Certain proteins in the goblet cells determine how thick and sticky *(viscosity)* and how stretchy *(elasticity)* the mucus is. Mucus is usually very watery but it gets thicker and stickier when exposed to irritants such as allergens, infections and pollution. In addition, hydration, age, hormones and medications affect the consistency of mucus. Older people experience thicker and stickier mucus because of hormonal changes, as do pregnant women.

During cold weather, the nose hairs do not work as well to sweep the mucus towards the back of the throat and this explains why we often develop a runny nose when exposed to very cold temperatures. Mucus also thickens in cold weather. When an individual comes in from the cold, the mucus thins and begins to run before the cilia begin to work again.

Mucus entraps irritants and protects our entire airway before being expelled. There are two layers in the mucous membrane lining of your nose. The outer layer is thick and rich with immune cells, antibodies, and antibacterial proteins. This layer traps bacterial, viral and particulate matter. The thinner, underlying layer enables the cilia to beat, their tips essentially grabbing the superficial layer and pushing it in the direction in which the cilia are beating, usually towards the back of the throat. Most normal mucus is swallowed and the trapped irritants are inactivated in the intestines (*gastrointestinal tract*) before leaving the body.

A problem occurs when mucus blocks the sinus or ear drainage openings. If the sinus opening (*ostiomeatal complex*) becomes plugged we are at risk for infection or at the very least a sinus pressure headache. Similarly, if the ear drainage tube (*Eustachian tube*) gets clogged, ear pain, decreased hearing, infection and other maladies can occur. When the normal flow of mucus is inhibited for any reason (*mucostasis*), dangerous bacterial, viral, or allergen particles can remain on cell surfaces long enough to penetrate the body's defense system.

Excess mucus draining down the throat is called *post-nasal drip*. This can cause a cough, a change in voice quality or a sore throat. Mucus is naturally acidic and can burn the throat if allowed to stagnate there. Hence, the complaint, "I woke up with a sore throat" is often a result of mucus drainage during sleep. Enough mucus and swelling can also cause a decreased sense of smell and taste.

The Wonders Of Mucus

- Goblet cells in the mucous membrane produce mucus
- Mucus is swept along by cilia
- Mucus protects cells and traps irritants
- Mucus is cleared by sneezing, coughing, swallowing, blowing
- Mucous membranes cover the entire respiratory and digestive tract lining
- Amount of mucus is increased when exposed to allergens, infections, pollutants
- Consistency of mucus thickness when exposed to allergens, infections, pollutants

Mucus And Its Many Colors:
'Help! My Mucus Is Green!'

In general, mucus is clear, thin and watery. If infected with virus, bacteria, or fungus particles, mucus normally changes to colors that can include white, yellow, green, brown, grey or even blood tinged. Often discolored mucus can have an offensive odor.

Many people assume that if their mucus is clear or white, they are not infected but if the mucus is yellow or green, they require an antibiotic. This is not true.

In fact, when one has a common cold, the mucus progresses from clear to white to yellow to green and sometimes grey or brown and then clears again, all within 7-10 days. If one has persistent (more than 3-5 days) yellow or green discharge, then a bacterial infection *may* be present. We now know that even if a bacterial infection is suspected, a good flushing may prevent the need for medications. Only about 20% of bacterial sinusitis cases actually require antibiotics. This is also true for inner ear infections. NOTE: The antibiotic may treat the infection but will not address the original cause of the unhealthy environment.

People with asthma experience excess mucus production as part of the asthma inflammatory reaction, particularly in the bronchial tubes but also in the nasal cavity. This mucus is usually white and frothy and blocks or clogs the airways which in turn causes chest tightness, coughing, and wheezing.

Mucus Serves As A Frontline Defense

- Filters and moisturizes our air
- Traps inhaled irritants (molds, pollen, dust mites, animal dander, smoke, ash, pollution)
- Protects against bacterial or viral invasion
- Contains bacteria-fighting substances, including natural antibodies
- Moistens food, making it easier to swallow and pass through the intestine
- Smoothes the airway's linings and traps foreign substances before they invade the lower respiratory system

The Cilia Sweep

Remember the little hairs (*cilia*) that blanket the inside of the nose and the sinuses? These are tiny projections which move in a wave-like pattern to transport mucus and all filtered material from the nose. Most mucus and debris are swallowed, spit out, or physically removed by blowing the nose.

I like to think of cilia as a broom because they function to sweep the mucus outward. The sinuses in their healthy state are relatively empty, thanks to the constant sweeping of the mucus against gravity. The cilia work in unison to move the mucus through the drainage openings (*ostia*). The mucus is drained into the nasal cavity where it then exits out of the nose or onto the back of the throat. When cilia do not function properly due to infection, smoking, or a congenital problem (rare), mucus is not properly cleared. Infection then becomes a self-perpetuating process during which the infected mucus interferes with the normal sweeping process of the cilia and this in turn prevents proper clearance of the mucus.

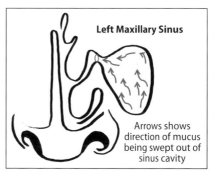

Left Maxillary Sinus

Arrows shows direction of mucus being swept out of sinus cavity

Summary Of Normal Functions

Cilia filter and mobilize
...debris, mucus, irritants, pollen, dust particles, virus, bacteria
Mucus traps
...particles and moistens membranes
Sinus and Ear Openings *(ostio)*
...allow normal mucus to drain from sinuses and ear cavities

Smell And Taste

Both of these senses are directly related to the health of the nose.

Smell *(Olfactory System)*

What would life be like without the ability to smell? The term *anosmia* means lack of or decreased sense of smell.

The olfactory nerve cells with their special ends, called *olfactory receptors*, are located at the upper area of each nasal cavity. This is why we sniff to increase the ability to smell subtleties. The average nasal cavity contains more than 100 million olfactory neurons. In newborns, the nerve endings are a compacted sheet, but in children and adults, these tissues become less dense and interwoven. As humans age, the number of olfactory neurons steadily decreases.

The sense of smell is initiated by airborne chemicals that enter the nasal cavity in circular currents of air movement. These chemicals stimulate our olfactory nerves. The response to an odor is directly related to the sniff's duration, volume and velocity. The ability to smell can be compromised if the olfactory receptors are covered in mucoid debris.

Taste *(Gustatory System)*

Considered the fifth sense, taste is mostly the smell of food in the mouth. *Ageusia* refers to a lack of or reduced ability to taste sweet, sour, bitter, or salty substances.

Taste buds are tiny projections embedded in the tongue; a single taste bud can respond to multiple types of tastes. Taste buds cover the tongue, but are also located on the soft palate, epiglottis, larynx and pharynx.

Certain tastes are appreciated by anatomical locations. For example, sweetness is most readily detected at the tip of the tongue, whereas salty taste is detected at the front and sides of the tongue. Sour tastes are along the sides and bitter sensations are appreciated at the back of the tongue.

In humans and many other vertebrates, the sense of taste collaborates with the sense of smell in the brain's perception of flavor. The gustatory system is intertwined with the olfactory system. That is to say, smell and taste are very closely related. Anyone who cannot smell appreciates the fact that his or her food tastes differently or does not have any flavor at all.

Moods

Smells and the ability of the nose to fully function can affect our mood. Remember the last time you were exposed to a foul order? Immediately there was a disgust or distaste for the source. Better yet, remember the last time you smelled something romantically delicious? Immediately it can be a sensual experience, which leads to many normal and delightful life activities. I am certain you can relate to a past experience when you were exposed to a scent which evoked childhood memories.

Sexuality

The nose contains tissue that is identical to our sexual organs' erectile tissue. The turbinates inside the nose contain large collapsible pockets of blood called *venous sinusoids*. These sinusoids become engorged and swell in response to irritants, resulting in decreased airflow. When you are exposed to any irritant, the instantaneous reaction causes the typical congested nose. Have you ever walked into an environment that contains strong irritants? Your nose instantly swells, feeling dried, stuffy, and blocked. *Immediately.* Like an erection.

Survival is based on the ability to smell. The concept of human pheromones, or sexual scents of attraction, has been debated and researched for years. Pheromones existence in humans may be in dispute but if you think about it, how often have you been turned off just by someone's smell, or the reverse, turned on by a subtle perfume?

If you're looking for the mate of your dreams, pheromones may contribute to this attraction. Our body odors, perceived as pleasant and sexy to another person, are part of a highly selective process. So, pay attention to those signals when looking for a mate!

There is still much to learn about these substances but we do know that the nose and sexual behavior are related.

Other Uses For Your Nose

On a lighter note, rubbing noses with someone you really like just wouldn't be the same without a nose, would it? What non-Eskimos call "Eskimo kissing" is loosely based on a traditional greeting and form of expressing affection, usually between family members and loved ones.

Finally, just think how hard it would be to keep your glasses in front of your eyes, not to mention how sore your ears would get, if you didn't have a nose.

Functions Of The Nose

- Filter the air we breathe
- Moisten the air we breathe
- Warm the air we breathe

Sinuses — What Are They And Why Do We Have Them?

The sinuses are air-filled pockets within the skull; one pair on each side of the nose — the maxillary sinuses — one pair just between and above the eyebrows — the frontal sinuses — and a pair behind the nasal cavity, the spenoids. The ethnoids can vary in number from 6-12 sinus cavities on each side.

The function of the sinuses has been the subject of extensive research with still much to learn. What we do know is that the sinuses contribute to conditioning the air we breathe, give resonance to the voice, assist in absorbing shock, reduce the weight of the skull and contribute to facial growth. If we did not have sinuses, our skulls would be too heavy to carry around; they lighten our load and influence our facial form.

Sinus Drainage Outlet
Ostiomeatal Complex Turbinate

Maxillary
Sinus
Outflow

Stagnation – Mucus Blocked

Mucus

The *ostiomeatal complex* (OMC) is not merely just the sinus drainage area. It is one of the critical areas of the sinonasal network as it relates to infections. The OMC specifically involves the drainage pathway from the maxillary sinus into the meatus (the space lying under the middle turbinate) and the largest of the anterior ethmoid cells. This very essential position is precisely where most sinus infections begin, tucked between the lower two turbinates and emptying into the back of the throat.

There is a phenomenon called *stagnation* that can occur at the ostiomeatal complex — the main intersection of the drainage system. Stagnation occurs when the nose lining swells, blocking the ostiomeatal complex and disrupting normal mucus clearance. This results in an unhealthy sinus environment. Clearance of the nose is accomplished when free-flowing secretions, open draining ports, and freely moving cilia have been restored.

The sinuses, like the nose, secrete mucus and contain cilia. Interestingly, the nose contains many more mucus producing goblet cells than the sinuses, hence more production of snot. Of the various sinus cavities, the maxillary sinus has the most goblet cells.

The cilia present in the sinuses work to move mucus in wave-like sweeps outward, toward the opening. Sinus cilia beat at a rate of 700-800 beats per minute and move mucus at a rate of 9 mm per minute. The movement of mucus

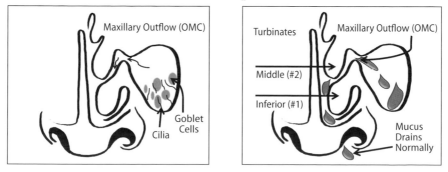

Maxillary Outflow (OMC)

Goblet
Cells
Cilia

Turbinates   Maxillary Outflow (OMC)

Middle (#2)

Inferior (#1)

Mucus
Drains
Normally

is known as *mucociliary clearance,* or transit time. This clearance is vital since some sinuses drain via an opening at the top rather than the bottom and the cilia must move mucus against gravity.

The sinuses drain into the ostiomeatal complex and if clear, will drain normally. If obstructed by disease or normal body variations, the sinuses are unable to move mucus out and thus congestion begins. This crucial location requires cleansing without disrupting the natural balance.

When all is working well, the sinuses are clear and empty of stagnant mucus.

Note: the exit (*maxillary outflow*) is small, located higher than the maxillary body and tucked between the turbinate folds. One can easily imagine how this becomes blocked due to colds, allergies, dried mucus and, as we will learn later, pregnancy.

As mentioned above, there are four pairs of sinuses in adults: *maxillary, frontal, ethmoid, and sphenoid.* Babies are born with two of these sinus sets, the maxillary and the ethmoid. The remaining two sets develop during childhood, starting in the first year and expanding progressively, and continue developing years after puberty.

Maxillary Sinuses

Sinus Drainage Outlet (OMC)

2.4 mm (less than ¼ inch)

Maxillary Sinuses

The largest of the sinuses are the maxillary, one located in each cheek. Imagine a cave-like room with the only window being at the very top of a wall, near the ceiling. This drainage port is higher than the body of the sinus. That means the cleansing sweep of the cilia must move **opposite** gravity.

The bony opening *(ostium)* size is very small, averaging 2.4 mm (a hair less than ¼ inch). The actual sinus opening is even narrower than the opening in the bone because the mucosa lining takes up space. Additionally, it is difficult for a doctor to see this tiny opening because it is hidden behind a bony protuberance. All of these factors contribute to a final sinus drainage port that is tiny and well hidden.

Frontal Sinuses

Frontal Sinuses

The frontal sinuses are located in the middle of the forehead. Unlike the maxillary cavities, they have their ostia at the bottom portion of the cavity, so they have gravity working for them. Accordingly, these sinuses are less likely to become infected.

Ethmoid Sinuses

The ethmoid sinuses are like sponges with tiny openings; this sponge is actually bone with many air cells. They are located at the roof of the nose, between the eyeballs. The bone is lightweight with approximately 6-12 small sinuses per side. The nerves (small fibers), which allow us to smell the world around us, are located on the nasal septum and the medial aspect of each middle and superior turbinate. These sinuses drain indirectly into the ostiomeatal complex.

Sphenoid Sinuses

Ethmoid Sinuses (closer to skin) Sphenoid Sinuses (deeper in the skull)

Located directly behind the ethmoid sinuses, the sphenoid sinuses are near the middle of the skull. These can vary in both shape and size. Often, the nasal septum can influence their contour. In fact, those with a deviated septum (a septum that is deviated a bit to one side) are more at risk of developing an infection in this particular cavity.

In general, a good washing of the nasal cavity is all that is needed to maintain a healthy environment for the tissues. Encouraging adequate drainage of the maxillary sinuses allows the natural process to proceed.

As The Nose Goes, The Ears Follow

Structure Of The Ear

We can't look inside our own ears but we can sure feel what goes on in there! As you will soon learn, what goes on in the ears is intimately connected to the nose. Three distinct areas make up the human ear: the outer, the middle, and the inner ear.

The "ear canal" is part of the outer ear. This is the part we can see, the part that can get blocked with ear wax, and the part that captures sound from outside the body. The ear canal carries sound to a thin translucent membrane called the eardrum, or the *tympanic membrane*. It is the only portion a medical provider can easily observe in a clinic setting when evaluating a possible ear infection.

On the other side of the tympanic membrane is the middle ear, an air-filled chamber that contains the *ossicles* (three tiny bones all linked together.) When the eardrum vibrates with sound coming from the ear canal, the ossicles pick up the vibrations and amplify them, carrying them to the inner ear. The inner ear translates those vibrations into electric signals and sends them to the auditory nerve, which is connected to the brain. When these nerve impulses reach the brain, they're interpreted as sound.

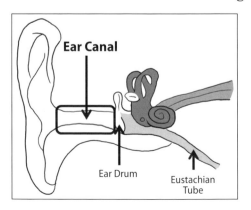

Ear Canal

Ear Drum

Eustachian Tube

So how does this involve the nose? Well, there is a direct

22

Middle Ear

Ossicles

Ear Drum   Eustachian Tube

Inner Ear

Auditory Nerve
Sends Signals
to Brain

Ear Drum

connection between the middle ear and the nose.

For sound vibrations to send the signals to the inner ear, the middle part of the ear must be ventilated, allowing the air pressure on either side of the tympanic membrane to equalize. The *Eustachian tube* is responsible for this ventilation. This tube begins in the middle ear and extends into the back of the upper throat, approximately at the same level as your nostrils. The portion of this tube nearest the eardrum is always open, protecting the middle ear. The end that drains into the back of the throat is normally closed. We open and close this part of the Eustachian tube when you move your jaw such as chewing, talking, sucking and especially yawning.

In adults, the Eustachian tube is approximately 35 mm long (1.38 inches). In children, it is significantly smaller and more difficult to drain for many reasons.

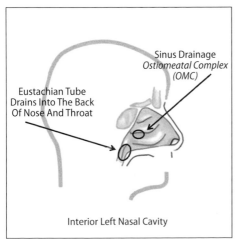

Eustachian Tube
Drains Into The Back
Of Nose And Throat

Sinus Drainage
Ostiomeatal Complex
(OMC)

Interior Left Nasal Cavity

Eustachian
Tube

Eustachian Tubes Differ Between Kids And Adults

	Kids	Adults
Size of passageway	Smaller	Larger
Direction of drainage into throat	Horizontal	More vertical, assisted by gravity
Stiffness of tube	Softer, therefore collapsible	Stiffer
Length of tube	Shorter (9mm, 0.35 inches)	Longer (18mm, 0.71 inches)
Opening into throat	Rounder	Oblong

When Your Eustachian Tube Doesn't Work

We all have experienced the sensation of the ear popping or pain when we fly or dive. In order to function properly, and without pain or pressure, the middle ear must be at the same pressure as the outside world. This equalization of pressure occurs via the open passage created by the Eustachian tube from the middle portion of the ear to the back of the throat, behind the nose. When the ears "pop" while yawning or swallowing or changing altitudes, the Eustachian tubes are adjusting the air pressure in your middle ears. Simply put, an air bubble travels upward in the tube. This is a good sign that at least the tube is not 'glued' shut. Doctors often use the term 'glue' ears because the body's reaction to chronic inflammation can result in a substance around the ossicles that prevent normal function.

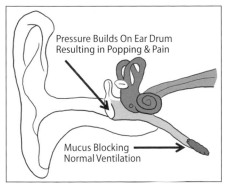

Pressure Builds On Ear Drum Resulting in Popping & Pain

Mucus Blocking Normal Ventilation

The Eustachian tube also drains mucus from the middle ear. Upper airway infections or allergies can cause this tiny tube to become swollen, trapping bacteria and causing middle ear infections.

If air is bubbling up and mucus is flowing down and out into the throat, all is well. But for this to happen it is vital that the Eustachian tube remain open and free to drain. None of this can be accomplished if there is a mucus plug or if there is swelling, as both prevent natural drainage.

Again, as the nose goes, the ears follow. Nasal health is critical for healthy ears.

The Eyes Have It —
An Intimate Connection With The Nose

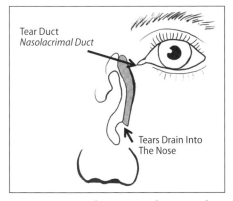

Tear Duct
Nasolacrimal Duct

Tears Drain Into The Nose

The tear duct (*nasolacrimal duct*) drains tears from the eyes and empties those tears under the lowest turbinate. This is why crying often results in nasal discharge. This also explains why nasal washing done incorrectly can push the solution up and out through the tear ducts.

This pathway may contribute to allergens entering the eyes, draining into the nose and causing allergic symptoms in the nose. There is also evidence that there may be backward (*retrograde*) flow from the nose back up into the eyes as well. For example, if you're wearing goggles but are exposed to outdoor pollen, you might develop itchy eyes. The pollen has entered the nose but because of the retrograde movement of the pollen, the eyes may itch. This is another example of how the individual parts of our facial anatomy are all connected.

CHAPTER 2

Paying Through The Nose —
The Cost Of Nasal Woes

 The numbers are always changing, and they are *not* going down. Americans spend billions of dollars every year treating nasal, allergy, sinus, ear and asthma problems. The dollars spent are only part of the price tag. The cost in terms of time off work, away from school, sitting in a doctor's office and just time spent feeling lousy is sky-high. How about time spent in the bathroom dealing with side effects of a medication? What about lost sleep, lack of focus and impatience with family and co-workers?

The point is, if your nose isn't working properly you are losing time and money, as well as impacting your quality of life. You are, quite literally, paying through the nose. Consider these figures, just a sampling of the numbers illustrating the annual cost of nose woes:

- Billions of dollars spent on medicine and treatment for allergic rhinitis
- Over 25 million Americans suffer from hay fever symptoms
- The majority of all antibiotic prescriptions are written to treat respiratory infections
- Billions of dollars spent on the evaluation and treatment of ear infections
- Quality of life is significantly reduced for those who suffer from hay fever
- Asthma is the most common cause of school absenteeism due to chronic conditions
- Billions of dollars spent to treat asthma
- Children typically have 2-9 viral respiratory illnesses

Childhood asthma prevalence more than doubled from 1980 to the mid-1990s and remains at historically high levels. The factors driving this pattern are still not fully understood.[1,2] Contributing factors include increased pollution, processed foods, and in general, unhealthy lifestyles.

Asthma is one of the leading chronic childhood diseases in the United States and a major cause of childhood disability.[3,4]

Okay, that's the bad news. The good news is you don't have to just suffer and spend money. You can do something to treat both the symptoms and the cause of these conditions. Let's see what an expert has to say about this situation.

Special Section: Let's Hear From The Experts

Marilyn James-Kracke, PhD is an associate professor of medical pharmacology and physiology. She teaches students preparing for careers in medicine, pharmacology and nursing; she is an expert on drugs! Her comments are based on her knowledge and personal experience.

Green Health Care (Prevention vs. Treatment)

Sick days cost the American economy billions per year. Lost work days stress both employers and employees. For those without substitutes to fill in, the thought of becoming ill invokes panic. To cope, they take extra precautions to stay well. I am one of those "solo" workers. I try to remain in tiptop shape by washing my nose twice daily.

I look upon my classroom as a microcosm of society because the pharmaceutical industry, health care industry and the population of this country affect topics we discuss. By allowing my imagination free reign, I can foresee industry, business, politics and finance benefiting if society assumes responsibility to reduce health care costs. Can nose washing help to cap these costs to improve the well-being of the nation? Permit me to expound on this topic.

Teachers benefit if children are not sneezing and coughing throughout class. Words of wisdom are more audible when there is no din of bark-bark-barkers, ha-ha-chachoo-ers and foghorn nose blowers. For daycare teachers, wiping noses of toddlers is an occupational hazard. School aged children blow their own noses with variable degrees of success but still innocently spread airborne pathogens to menace everyone sharing the same air.

Since not breathing is not an option, flushing nasal germs down the drain to deplete their virulence makes more sense to reduce absenteeism. Do you remember substitute teachers who provided comic relief from an ogre-ish one? That was fun, but we learned little that day. It was a hardship when excellent teachers were absent or mothers collapsed in their line of duty. Working mothers should view nose washing as job and salary protection insurance.

Wherever people gather in confined spaces, they contract airborne illness. Planes, trains and buses are common perpetrators of germ warfare. How many people frugally save for a special vacation only to become sick as a dog while traveling? Think of nose washing as a form of travel insurance.

What are our alternatives? Should we wear facemasks to prevent the spread of illness? We expect everyone to be vaccinated and toilet-trained, wash their hands, sneeze into tissues, brush their teeth and shower. Has the time come to add nose washing to standard daily hygiene?

What do I want to achieve? My intentions are to:

Encourage the reduction of suffering and reduce the spread of illness to immune compromised patients like the elderly, infants and those undergoing chemotherapy

Make schools healthier learning environments

Make workplaces healthier and workforces more productive

Lower the cost of healthcare that is bankrupting the economy

Americans must "save for a rainy day." Saving trees by reducing tissue use is a good idea too. Nasal washing reduces the need for certain drugs and hospital treatments. Given a choice between washing my nose for a minute a day and being congested perpetually all day I will wash my nose. We must demonstrate that nose washing does not cause drowning or even discomfort.

Marilyn James-Kracke, PhD
Associate Professor of Medical Pharmacology & Physiology
Department of Medical Pharmacology & Physiology
School of Medicine, University of Missouri

CHAPTER 3

Medications

Medications & Additives For The Nose: Used, Misused, Abused

 No one would dispute the miracles of modern medicine: the surgeries performed through tiny openings, organ transplants and re-attachment of limbs, the advance of chemotherapy and the many lives antibiotics have saved. People would be best served if modern medicine would incorporate patient education, nutrition, and prevention, as well as complementary and alternative approaches. My personal perspective on medication use comes from this position: Do I really need the drug? Are other options available? Would I give this to my child or to my mother? Is this one of those drugs currently approved by the governmental regulatory agencies but that will, in time, be found to cause more harm than good?

There is no doubt the nose requires moisture for proper functioning. Things go wrong if the nose is dry. Nasal saline alone may not be enough and there are some safe additives. These can include potassium chloride, calcium chloride, sodium bicarbonate, and hydrogen peroxide.

But there are nasal medications that are not without risk, some of which are easily abused. Let's look at a few common problematic medications.

Nasal Medications, Preservatives & Additives

 Nasal sprays are easy to use, but there is evidence that many of the preservatives and additives in some of the commercial nasal sprays can be harmful to the nose!

Some additives I like to avoid include benzyl alcohol, providone, iodine, disodium ETA, edetate disodium, benzalkonium, thimerosal, merthiolate, monobasic sodium phosphate, dibasic sodium phosphate, potassium phosphate monobasic, phenylcarbinol, and sodium silicoaluminate. Some of these can directly irritate the sensitive lining of the nose, and some can cause allergic reactions. Maybe it's a good rule of thumb to avoid putting in your nose any substance you cannot pronounce!

More warnings:

- Some topical nasal decongestants contain sulfites. Asthmatics may react to sulfites, and some of these reactions may be life threatening.

- Do not use nasal spray decongestants in children younger than 2 years old because these medications can interact with oral decongestants in cold medications.

- The nasal medications which contain benzalkonium chloride (BKC), a preservative that prevents the growth of microorganisms, can cause more rebound swelling than those that are BKC free. Thus, BKC may aggravate a condition known as Rhinitis Medicamentosa (RM, or nasal spray addiction, see below.)

Nasal Spray Addiction: *Rhinitis Medicamentosa*

Rhinitis Medicamentosa (RM) is a fancy name for physical addiction to a nasal spray. It is "rebound nasal congestion" caused directly by overuse and abuse of intranasal decongestants. These medications are vasoconstrictive, which means they close down blood vessels.

It continues to be unclear how decongestant nasal sprays cause the classic rebound swelling of RM, wherein congestion is worse after the effect of the spray wears off. What is clear is that the longer you use these sprays, the more often dosing is required to achieve the same benefit. In addition, when you try to quit using the medication, your nose reacts by becoming more swollen and congested than it was to begin with.

As a consequence of prolonged use of nasal decongestants, RM often leads to mucous membranes that are very abnormal in both appearance and function. They can appear very red, irritated and swollen with areas that easily bleed. Some reports suggest that the lining of the nose appears pale and anemic. The mucus is usually clear and minimal, unless an accompanying sinus infection is present. Others report profuse and thick mucus. In either case, the tissues are unhealthy and not able to function properly.

Because of the abuse of nasal decongestants, chronic sinusitis, chronic runny nose due to thinning of the nasal membranes and permanent turbinate hyperplasia (development of excessive tissue inside the nose) can result. The cost of treating these side effects is considerably higher than the price of the medication.

Decongestants

 Many of us have reached for a decongestant when we are congested and stuffy. The active ingredient used in many over the counter decongestants, phenylephrine, is used to relieve nasal or sinus congestion caused by the common cold, sinusitis, hay fever and other respiratory irritants. This medicine and other similar drugs relieve stuffy noses, open nasal airways, and allow sinuses to drain. It is also used to relieve ear congestion caused by inflammation or infection.

This type of drug does decongest, but its use also comes with potential risks. Have you ever felt the jitters after taking this medicine? That's because it is a stimulant, with side effects which are potentially serious.

Serious reactions include heart arrhythmias and severe hypertension. More commonly, people who take this medication can experience insomnia, nausea, headaches, dizziness, nervousness, irritability, heart palpitations, weakness or tremors. There are specific warnings for women who are pregnant, for small children, and for people taking other medications. It is so easy to take a little tiny decongestant pill and then go on with your day. But before you do, inform yourself about what you are putting into your body.

So if a decongestant is worrisome, what choices do you have for that itchy, drippy, sneezy or stuffy nose? The safest, simplest option is a salty nose wash, which acts as a natural decongestant. Salty nose washes (hypertonic buffered saline) work to shrink swollen membranes naturally, without harmful side effects.

Antihistamines

What Are Antihistamines And How Do They Work?

If you have allergies and are exposed to an irritant such as a pollen particle, a chemical called *histamine* is released from the body's cells. This chemical causes itching, sneezing, runny noses and watery eyes. Antihistamines prevent or reduce the symptoms caused by histamines. So antihistamines can treat *some* of the symptoms of allergies, colds, and reactions to insect bites, stings, and poison ivy/oak.

Antihistamines cross into the brain and affect that portion of the brain which controls nausea and vomiting, so they are also used to treat motion sickness. In addition, some of the earlier first generation antihistamines cause sleepiness and can be effectively used to treat insomnia.

Side Effects Of Antihistamines

There are two types of over-the-counter (OTC) antihistamines which can be purchased without a doctor's prescription: first generation and the newer, second generation antihistamines.

Best-known of the first generation OTC antihistamines is diphenhydramine, in Benadryl. Others include brompheniramine in Dimetapp, and chlorpheniramine and dimenhydrinate in Dramamine, just to name a few.

These all tend to cause sedation but approximately 10-15% of people, particularly children, can have an opposite reaction and become stimulated (hyperactive, unable to sleep, or irritable). Only a trial of these medications will tell what kind of a responder you or your child may be.

When first-generation antihistamines make you feel sleepy, they adversely affect your ability to drive, operate machines, pay attention and think clearly. A 2000 study published in the *Annals of Internal Medicine* compared the effects of diphenhydramine and alcohol on driving response times. The conclusion stated "… diphenhydramine had a greater impact on driving than alcohol did." These first generation antihistamines can also cause dry mouth, dry eyes, and thickened mucus, which may increase the risk of developing a sinus infection.

Second generation antihistamines (Claritin, Allegra, Zyrtec, and generic loratadine) are *usually* non-sedating. However, each person is unique and some people do complain of sedating side effects with the newer products. These tend to have a longer lasting effect, up to 24 hours, unlike the first generation antihistamines which typically last 4-6 hours.

You should be aware that antihistamines are often combined with other drugs like decongestants, pain relievers, and mucus thinners (mucolytics). If you buy a pre-mixed combination, the risk of mixing two types of the same medication rises. Antihistamines can also interact with many other over-the-counter and prescription medications. This is particularly true in children and the elderly but it is not an uncommon event in the general population. Some antihistamines interact with other drugs by changing the way your body processes or clears the drug from your body, so beware before you mix antihistamines with sleeping pills, muscle relaxants, or high blood pressure medications. In my practice, my preference and recommendation is to avoid the trap of convenience and use only those individual medications which you clearly want or need.

Talk to your physician before taking first generation antihistamines if you have glaucoma, an enlarged prostate gland, asthma, emphysema, chronic bronchitis, thyroid disease, heart disease or high blood pressure. If you have liver or kidney disease, be careful and check with your doctor before using second generation antihistamines.

Other Medications

There are scores of other medications available and often used for nasal woes. For the sake of completeness, I list some of the familiar ones here. Each medication has its place but also its potential ill effects. Just remember: stay informed and choose wisely.

- Mucolytics (in Mucinex, generic guainefesin) — medications which thin mucus and other secretions — one of my favorites.

- Cough suppressants (codeine, dextromethorphan) — inhibit the brain's reflex to cough — useful only on a very short term basis and usually best used at night to get some healing sleep. Recently, researchers have found that cough suppressants are no more effective in relieving children's nighttime coughs than placebos are, so pediatricians recommend avoiding their use in those younger than six years old. And remember: Never 'hide' a chronic cough unless you know the cause.

- Nasal steroids including Flonase, Nasonex, Rhinocort — inhibit the body's immune response to irritants. They have a long list of potential side effects, including the encouragement of fungal overgrowth, but can be helpful if applied to clean nasal membranes.
- Nasal antihistamines (Astelin) — few worrisome side effects. Applying this drug onto clean tissues is most effective.
- Immune modulators (cromolyn sodium, Singular) — halt the allergic response in a different pathway compared to antihistamines. Treats the symptoms and the body's response to allergens, but does not address the root of the problem.
- Antibiotics — attempt to treat the infection but do nothing for the original cause of the infection. Overuse is problematic, expensive and has risks. Often infections will resolve without the antibiotics.
- Asthma medications (inhaled anti-inflammatories, bronchial dilators) — have numerous side effects, but can be lifesaving. There exists a wealth of knowledge that addressing nose and sinus problems (nasal washing as a first line) reduces the need for asthma medications.

From The Expert

Nasal steroids control symptoms caused by inflammation. The average benefit from this treatment is small but definite, and for some patients it may work especially well. Thus, a two-week therapeutic trial period is reasonable. If it is ineffective, it may work if tried again later. Although it can promote proliferation of yeasts and possibly other microbes, side effects are usually minor — perhaps mild nasal irritation or bleeding. Nasal steroids have a more definite benefit when there is nasal obstruction due to large adenoids. In adequate doses, a four to eight-week course can significantly reverse obstruction, sometimes enough to avoid surgery.

Michael Cooperstock, M.D., MPH
Division Chief, Pediatric Infectious Disease,
Immunology, & Rheumatology
Professor of Infectious Disease
Department of Child Health
School of Medicine, University of Missouri

" Avoided Decongestants

About a year ago I really needed some pseudoephedrine-type decon-
gestant and there was a long line at the pharmacy, so I ended up trying
a nose wash. I have used in regularly and have come to like it a lot. **" "**

Laura T., Grand Forks, Minnesota

" Family Affair

Nasal washing works. Everyone with allergies should do it. I don't
buy sinus medicine anymore, and I don't have headaches. **" "**

Dana M., Louisville, Kentucky

As I was completing work on this book I ran across an article in the *The Wall Street Journal*, entitled "Waiting it Out: Antibiotics Are Unlikely to Help Sinusitis."[5] Reporter Anna Wilde Mathews notes that antibiotics do little or no good in treating sinus infections and that, increasingly, doctors are turning to treatments that do not involve medications. This once again supports the recommendation that every sinus infection need not be treated with antibiotics.

A 2007 research study published in JAMA (*Journal of the American Medical Association*) reached the same conclusion.[6] This study reported that over-prescription of antibiotics can increase sinus infections' resistance to the drugs. The lead author of the study, Dr. Ian Williamson, said, "With a little bit of patience, the body will usually heal itself."

CHAPTER 4

Nasal Washing —
Dilution Is The Solution To The Pollution

 Nasal washing has finally become familiar to many consumers. Ten years ago, when I introduced the idea of irrigation, the majority of my patients never even considered the idea of washing the inside of the nose. Five years ago, the suggestion was considered a bit *on the edge*. Today, most people have at least heard or read about this common sense notion.

Why Has Nasal Washing Become So Popular?

- Complementary, alternative and integrative medicine has boomed in popularity
- Prevention is the new treatment
- Less aggressive approach is green and good for the environment
- Neti exposure from the "Oprah — Dr. Oz effect"
- Bacteria has developed resistance to antibiotics
- Recent press coverage on the overuse of antibiotics
- Press coverage of drug recalls, such as cold preparations for kids
- American Academy of Pediatrics new guidelines regarding cold medicines, ear infections and overuse of antibiotics
- Drug commercials with side effects of medications listed
- Costs of medications
- Internet information
- Consumers are asking for advice and people want to know
  - In 2000 Google search for "nasal irrigation" resulted in less than 100,000 responses
  - In 2005 Google search for "nasal irrigation" resulted in 800,000 responses
  - In 2008 Google search for "nose wash" resulted in 11.4 million responses

I have lectured to medical doctors, respiratory therapists, nurse practitioners, and many other health care providers. I am often surprised by how often the question, "Isn't this the same as a saline nasal spray?" is asked, but when you think about it, it becomes rather obvious that a small spritz is quite different than a full flush. When you develop an infected wound, your medical provider's first step is to flush the wound with sterile water, not simply spray or mist it. Then, and only then, is further treatment even considered. I propose the same approach be taken with nasal, sinus, and respiratory issues. It also occurs to me that the current western medicine focus is all too often on treatment rather than prevention.

Why Do Medical Providers Need To Know About Nasal Washing?

- To be able to offer it as a treatment option for their patients.
- To become familiar with current nasal washing devices and various solution ingredients.
- To understand what system would be best for their patients.
- To become comfortable enough to incorporate nasal washing into the art of medicine.
- To understand the limitations of nasal washing.

The History Of Nasal Irrigation

As early as 1882, western medical textbooks demonstrated nasal washing. Polish physician Alfred Laskiewicz, chief of Pozna Hospital Otolaryngology Department (1932-1939) described conservative treatments of nasal irrigation for general hygiene and for medical problems such as Scleroderma (a skin disease). The Proetz procedure has been used by ear, nose and throat surgeons for years to clean out the sinuses during surgery.

Nasal rinsing (*lavage*) devices have included gravity flow vessels, pressure bottles, IV bags, squirts, flushers, syringes, electric machines, squeeze bottles and turkey basters, among others. Some people mistakenly include misters, sprays and humidifiers among nasal irrigation devices but let's make this perfectly clear: **They are not**. One is a flowing cleansing flush, the other is a mild misting or spray.

Since the mid- to late 1990's, there has been a slow-growing interest in the idea of nasal cleansing. Since the new millennium, this interest has exploded, powered by the surge in the focus on prevention, alternatives, and an overall integrative approach to health. Well-known doctors have promoted the practice of nasal washing. Although antihistamines, decongestants, steroids and antibiotics are commonly prescribed, doctors have added the adjunctive treatment of nasal irrigation for allergy sufferers, post operative sinus surgery patients and for those who suffer from chronic sinusitis. I have been suggesting nasal washing for two decades now, but only recently has it been formally recommended as a mainstream preventative approach.

Special Section: Let's Hear From The Experts

I have asked **P. Leszek Vincent, Ph.D.**, for his perspective on the history and the origins of nasal washing. Dr. Vincent is a research professor who has studied traditional remedies through the ages and has considerable expertise in the history and use of medicinal plants. He has studied in South Africa, the United Kingdom and the United States and has written several publications on medicinal plants.

Nose Washing Through The Ages

Nasal washing, or nasal irrigation, is an ancient Ayurvedic technique known as Jala neti, which literally means "nasal cleansing" in Sanskrit (a classical language of South Asia). With origins based in the yoga tradition, nasal washing has been used throughout India and South East Asia. Although not commonly practiced by Western cultures, these Eastern cultures have performed Jala neti as routinely as brushing one's teeth for centuries. Yogic breathing practices, known as pranayama, are enhanced by the practice of jala neti since many of them involve deep breathing through the nostrils, and clear nasal passages permit deeper, more relaxed breathing.

Traditionally a neti pot, a vessel shaped like an Aladdin's lamp or teapot, has been used to flow salt water into one nostril, and out the other nostril. In addition to using the neti pot, ancient yogis experienced success by snorting salt water in a rhythmic fashion as part of their daily rituals.

In the West, doctors have known the benefits of nasal washing for more than a century. The first mention of nasal irrigation in western medical literature is in an article published in 1902 in the British medical journal The Lancet. This article also mentions the inclusion of "a pinch of sodium bicarbonate" to the warm saline solution as the bicarbonate can improve the quality of the cleansing action of the nasal wash solution. Interestingly this article also mentions the value of using boiled sea water as a nasal wash solution. Coastal cultures around the world provide much anecdotal information about the value of swimming in the sea or sniffing seawater up into the nose, when suffering from a cold or other nasal congestion problem. Note that the salt content of seawater is approximately 3.5% while that of a hypertonic saline solution, typically used in current nasal washing practice, ranges from 3 to 5%. Recent medical research has demonstrated that nasal irrigation using a hypertonic saline solution promotes the body's cleaning of the mucus membranes in our noses, via stimulating the cleaning action of the minute hairs that are found on the surface of the mucous membranes in our nasal passages (mucociliary clearance). It is interesting that the human practice of nasal washing, while having ancient roots, is founded upon sound medical and scientific principles.

P. Leszek Vincent, PhD, FLS
Research Assistant Professor
Division of Plant Sciences
University of Missouri

The Evolution Of Nose Washing Devices

Device	Description	Flow	Date
	Dr. Sage's Nasal Douche	Gravity	1890s
	Glass Bottle with air port	Gravity	1902
	Upright Vessel	Gravity	1915
	Double Portal	Gravity	1917
	Benjamin Nasal Douche	Gravity	1930s
	Neti - Aladdin Device	Gravity	At Least three millennium

The Evolution Of Nose Washing Devices, *continued*

Device	Description	Flow	Date
	Upright bottle	Gravity	~ 2000
	Squeeze bottle with billow	Positive pressure, against gravity	1990s
	Squeeze bottle with straw	Positive pressure, against gravity	2000
	Squeeze bottle with straw	Positive pressure, against gravity	2006
	Squeeze bottle	Gravity & positive pressure	2004
	Syringe	Positive Pressure, against gravity	~ 2000
	Pulsating Mechanical Irrigation	Forced pressure	~ 2000

CHAPTER 5

The Ins And Outs Of Nasal Washing — Taking Care Of Your Great Defender

 Nasal washing is easily learned and just like most skills, becomes easier with practice. It is not difficult to master, and when performed correctly, it is a refreshing and soothing experience. It is analogous to brushing your teeth, flossing, or learning to use contact lenses.

Let's be clear here: nasal "irrigation" systems ARE NOT: sprayers, sniffing water, misters, nebulizers, gels, humidifiers, bulb syringes (mold grows easily inside these) or other devices that spray or moisturize only. Nor can nasal washing be accomplished by 'snorting' water into the nose.

Why Wash Daily?

- Daily practice of washing improves both nasal and sinus health
- Washes out thick and sticky mucus
- Thins thick and sticky secretions
- Reduces nasal congestion
- Improves air flow
- Improves filter efficiency
- Allows the sinus cavities to drain freely
- Removes allergens, irritants, bacteria, viruses and contaminants
- Helps reduce upper respiratory infections like the common cold
- May reduce dependency on medications (antibiotics, antihistamines, nasal steroids, decongestants, asthma medications)
- Relieves nasal dryness
- Can improve sense of smell

- Can improve sense of taste
- Helps to treat sinusitis and rhinitis
- Reduces allergic rhinitis symptoms
- Reduces coughing and other symptoms of post-nasal drip
- May reduce snoring
- May reduce nose bleeds
- Helps heal raw or irritated nasal membranes
- Clears airways affected by nose woes associated with pregnancy and maturity
- Helps clear excessive mucus caused by medical conditions such as Cystic Fibrosis
- Cleanses the nasal tissues stressed by radiation therapy to the head and sinus area
- Removes pollutants from the upper airway to allow deeper, more relaxed breathing
- Feels soothing & refreshing; *a shower for the nose*
- It's easy, inexpensive and makes sense

Who Should Wash?

Now, who should wash their nose? Well, consider this: Who should brush their teeth? People with teeth, right? The simple answer is, just about anyone who has a nose should wash their nose, and I'm being serious. Beyond this broad group, people who have particular concerns will appreciate dramatic benefits from daily nose washing. I'm talking about people who have:

- Sinus issues
- Nose issues
- Throat issues
- Asthma
- Post nasal drip (PND)

- Allergies
- Ear infections
- Sinus surgery/nasal surgery
- Irritating or non-allergic rhinitis (chemical or other airborne irritant to the nose)
- Seasoned noses
- Cystic Fibrosis (CF)
- Lack of or decreased sense of smell or taste
- Bad breath (from excessive infected mucus)
- Snoring issues
- Pregnancy rhinitis
- CPAP users, for sleep apnea

As well as

- Athletes, including but not limited to runners, football players, baseball players, soccer players, golfers, scuba divers, horseback riders
- Farmers & gardeners
- Travelers
- Workers in environments with poor or potentially harmful air quality such as firefighters, construction workers, painters, military personnel
- People who live in polluted cities
- Those interested in using fewer drugs and saving money
- Anyone interested in prevention: cleaning their personal filter

And that's just a partial list. Simply said:
Nasal Issues? Wash the tissues!

Who Should NOT Wash?

When I became a physician I took an oath to "First, do no harm." So I must tell you there are some people who should *not* use nasal irrigation:

- Those who are unable to stand alone and brush their teeth
- Anyone who can't follow instructions
- Those who have had recent trauma or surgery to the head or neck
- Anyone with a physician who says, "NO nasal washing for you!"
- Anyone who is being forced to use a nasal wash against their will

When To Wash?

- Allergy Season
- Cold & flu season for prevention
- At the first sign of nasal congestion
- Immediately after exposure to irritants and pollutants
- If infected in the ears, sinus, nose or throat
- During asthma flare-ups
- When your sense of smell and/or taste is impaired
- Before use of nasal steroids or other nasal medications
- Before using CPAP machines for sleep apnea
- Every day as part of general hygiene practice

How Frequently To Wash?

This depends on your need. These are my general guidelines:

For Prevention:
  Wash once per day or after exposure to irritants.

For Mild to Moderate Congestion or Discharge:
  Wash twice per day.

For Moderate to Severe Congestion, Discharge or Infection:
  Wash up to four times per day.

What To Wash With?

There are two qualities in a nasal rinse solution that make an enormous difference: **Salt concentration** and **acidity**. Our mucous membranes and the mucus produced in the nose are both naturally salty; an effective wash will take that saltiness into account. In addition, if the solution washing over the membranes is too acidic it will be irritating rather than soothing to the membranes. These factors are quite important, so we are going to take some time to explore both of them.

" Improved Performance

I have been a runner all of my life. In fact, I earned a college scholarship because of my running. I have always suffered with allergies, beginning with allergy shots at an early age and almost daily medications. Then my boyfriend came home one day with a nose wash in hand and said, "You have to try this". I was speechless as I stared at this crazy man! For starters, I had no idea what he was talking about, 'a nose wash?' Even after he showed me how to use it properly, it looked awkward and I had hesitations. He told me that washing my nasal passages would help my allergies and improve my performance as a runner. It was hard to turn something down that might help me succeed with my athletic career. I was also tired of taking antihistamines daily as well as antibiotics every few months. My nose was always stuffy, my head was always full. I told him that I would try it, only because I was desperate for some relief, so I was even willing to try this awkward weird new thing. The first time I used Nasopure was like nothing I had ever experienced. After daily washing for 2 weeks, I was actually amazed at how good I felt since I had been skeptical, to say the least. It did not cure my allergies, but it helped me breathe and breathing easier was a great thing. Because I am now able to breathe deeply and naturally, I can now focus on my running career. I am now medication free, breathing deeper, and running harder. "

Stefanie K. Lasley, RN, University of Missouri
Columbia, Missouri

" Cleaner!

I could immediately tell a difference in my nose, feeling just clearer to breathe after one use! I thought my whole family needed to try this. "

Paul Kute, Wichita, Kansas

" Gift Of Clean Air

Both my mother and dad love nose washing. They got theirs for Christmas and Mom says it is the best thing ever invented. "

Michelle B., Homecare Specialist
Morrisville, North Carolina

50

From The Expert

The frequency of nasal washing with buffered hypertonic nasal saline irrigation *is related to the severity of the disease. Patients with mild disease can irrigate only as needed for comfort. Patients with severe disease should irrigate three to four times each day or even more. The duration of nasal washings in days or weeks or months also depends on the severity of the disease and contributing factors such as allergies, colds, frequency of being around smokers, etc.*

David S. Parsons, M.D., FAAP, FACS
Clinical Professor, Universities of North & South Carolina
Pediatric Otolaryngology, Charlotte Eye, Ear, Nose and Throat

Solutions And Salt Facts You Should Know

Before we discuss salt concentrations, we need to review some basic physiology. The body has membranes that allow water to cross from one side to the other and as a result, we experience shrinking and swelling of those membranes. The diffusion or natural movement of water across a membrane is called *osmosis.*

When a permeable membrane like we have in our nose is washed with salty solution, the high salt content draws the excess liquid from the less salty side into the more salty side, in an attempt to equalize the concentration of salt on each side. Water moves through osmosis towards the highest salt content, coming out of the mucous membranes and, in effect, shrinking those membranes down.

When salt is concentrated inside or outside the cell membranes, it will draw the water in its direction.

Here's a good example of this phenomenon: Have you ever made coleslaw out of cabbage? Cabbage salad is best when crispy, not soggy. My mother knew that the way to make good coleslaw was to shred the cabbage and then cover it with liberal amounts of salt. When she returned a few minutes later to rinse the salted and shredded cabbage she knew that the bowl would be full of water. This water was the fluid extracted from the cabbage, leaving it crunchy and perfect for a salad.

Salt absorbs, it draws, it drinks, it extracts, and it sucks the water from its surroundings. In our nose there is evidence that salty solutions pull liquid out of swollen tissue, thus unplugging the sinus and inner ear openings, resulting in natural draining of mucus. Salty solutions also transform thick sticky mucus into a thinner consistency making drainage easier.

Saline is a generic term referring to salt and water. But this term does not reflect how many salt particles are in a given volume of water, i.e. the strength of the saline. The strength of saline is referred to as *tonicity*. Saline can be hypertonic, isotonic or hypotonic.

The body is the standard against which we gauge other salt mixtures; the salt concentration in the body is 0.9%. If a solution is identical to the salt concentration in the body, it is referred to as *isotonic*. If there is more salt as compared to the body, the solution is *hypertonic* and if there is less salt than the body it is *hypotonic*. The differences are amazing and worth understanding in detail.

Hypertonic

Hypertonic means the salt solution is saltier than the body's natural state.

Scientific studies support that hypertonic solution used as a nasal wash has numerous benefits:

- Shrinks
- Improves mucus flow
- Thins thick sticky secretions
- Improves the filtering efficiency of the nose
- Washes out irritants that cause allergies
- Is as safe as ocean water
- Can improve both sense of smell and bad breath
- Reduces the need for some medications when used on a regular basis
- Reduces the frequency of the common cold if used regularly

TONICITY: Salt Concentration

Hypotonic (Less than body) Hypertonic (More than body)

Isotonic (Same as the human body)

We also know this: a high salt, hypertonic concentration inhibits and kills viruses and bacteria. Washing the nasal cavities with a salty solution after exposure to a cold, or when fighting an infection has been shown to reduce the number of infectious particles. A hypertonic solution impedes infectious particles attempting to invade mucous membranes. It also reduces viral multiplication.

Sometimes washing with a hypertonic solution can be irritating to the nasal mucosa. I believe this experience can be related to several factors which include age, hormone levels, medication effects, and nasal history. This irritation is almost always temporary.

From The Expert

How effective Buffered Hypertonic Nasal Saline Irrigation is largely depends on the mechanism by which it is administered and the patient's motivation for getting well. Patients who are not motivated to optimally care for themselves seldom do as well. Patients with a strong desire for healing will aggressively seek the optimal irrigating instrument and continually wash the inside of their nose. Motivated patients require less medicine and less surgery to gain an acceptable cure.

David S. Parsons, M.D., FAAP, FACS
Clinical Professor, Universities of North & South Carolina
Pediatric Otolaryngology, Charlotte Eye, Ear, Nose and Throat

Special Section: Let's Hear From The Experts

Dr. Ben Francisco, a nurse practitioner who practices in a large teaching hospital, specializes in pediatric allergy and asthma as well as caring for those with Cystic Fibrosis. His experience includes decades of medical practice with a keen interest in prevention as well as treatments. Dr Francisco has become a leader in this field and lectures extensively to doctors, nurses, and respiratory therapists, with a focus on prevention.

Use of hypertonic nasal rinses has reduced the need for more invasive and risky treatments in our clinical practice. When the nose is in good condition it is protective against a range of other problems, including worsening asthma, shortness of breath with exertion related to nasal obstruction, and the development of bacterial infections in the sinuses.

Those who master good technique have great results and do not feel like rinsing the nose is a problem. On the other hand, those who do not master good technique often feel that this is a terrible thing to have to do. In my clinical practice I have parents with children as young as three years of age that tell me their child brings their rinse bottle to their mother saying that they want to rinse their nose. Then we have, of course, teens that run screaming when they see the rinse bottle.

I consider it important to introduce the technique in a way that is acceptable, giving people a clear mental image of what they are doing. The method that I currently use emphasizes that when you rinse your nose the most important thing is to first establish an air stream out of the free nostril before you squeeze the bottle and push a column of water into the other nostril. Failure to provide a ready outlet for the incoming stream of salt water can cause unpleasant effects including gagging and possible ear pain, because increased pressure in the throat is transmitted to the Eustachian tube and middle ear. I also find it helpful if the head is tilted forward so that the nostril receiving the water is above the nostril that is blowing the water out. I explain, "The air will lead the water back out of your nose."

Very young children present a special challenge to parents. However, if a child can blow their nose, I think they can easily adapt to the nasal rinsing technique described above. I use this method in clinic. Starting with air only I demonstrate the technique with young children and youths, asking that they lean forward and blow air slowly out of one nostril while I puff a little air from the irrigation bottle into the other nostril. We switch sides and repeat the procedure. I explain that practicing with air will make it easier to master the real thing at home with salt water.

I think it's also important to explain that use of hypertonic saline is like swimming in the ocean and having some salt water washing in and out of the nostrils. I compare rinsing the nose with salt water to swimming in the ocean — except we are bringing the ocean to you in a small bottle.

It is also helpful to understand that inside each nostril are three nasal turbinates. If the first turbinate is enlarged, then nasal steroids or nasal antihistamine sprays will not enter the upper nasal passages effectively. Instead, medication will strike the first turbinate and then flow back out, failing to have any impact on the other two turbinates or the lining of the upper nasal passages. This is confirmed by anecdotal reports by families and children in my practice when they say, "My medicine is not going in. It just streams back out of my nose even if I try to inhale or sniff it into the back of my nose." Rinsing the nose with hypertonic salt water before using the spray decongests and shrinks the turbinates, thus improving delivery of nasal medications.

Salt-water rinses also wash away secretions and debris (pollen, dust and other stuff in the air we breathe) that are contributing to nasal congestion. This is a common problem for school age children who play outdoors after school during mold and pollen season. When they come indoors, if the nose is doing its job, there is a considerable amount of allergen particles (spores or pollen) in the nose. If these are rinsed out it is likely that this will lessen the allergic response. Walking around with this stuff in your nose for hours cannot be a good thing.

A final effect, and in my mind the most important benefit of salt-water rinses, is stimulation of the natural sweepers that line the sinus passages. This effect results in improved mucociliary clearance, the natural system for washing the sinuses clear by moving secretions out of the nasal airways.

As an adjunct to treating sinus infections, nasal rinses with hypertonic salt water are valuable. People recover more quickly and are more likely to have a complete cure, even when antibiotics are also indicated. Future sinus infections might be averted and the need for antibiotics avoided if the person is comfortable using salt water rinses to aid body defenses in the future.

I am so convinced of the benefit of hypertonic salt-water rinses that I provide starter kits at no cost to families (hundreds of kits over the course of the last four years). I tell families that if they begin to rinse the nose for a period of a week or so when nasal congestion first occurs, there is a strong possibility that antibiotics may not be needed next time. I generally recommend a one-week period of daily nasal rinsing once or twice a day, preferably twice. I am more inclined to recommend rinsing the nose twice a day if the nasal symptoms are more severe or if they are not improving with once daily rinsing. Some people ask if they can rinse more often and the answer is yes.

I hope more will acquire this skill and use nasal rinsing as a routine part of their hygiene and wellness.

Benjamin Francisco, PhD, PNP, AE-C
Research Assistant Professor, Family Nurse Practitioner
Division of Pediatrics, Pulmonary, Allergy, and Cystic Fibrosis
Department of Child Health
School of Medicine, University of Missouri

Isotonic

Isotonic means the concentration of salt is equal on both sides of a membrane. When the body's salt concentration is the same as the washing solution, the solution will not have any effect on the overall amount of water on either side of the mucus membrane. Thus, this will not shrink swollen membranes. An isotonic concentration of salt solution can physically remove some irritants, but will not inhibit infections or thin the secretions. Some prefer the isotonic solution; it is a milder mix and feels comfortable when used daily but does not have as many benefits as hypertonic saline. Many people like to begin nasal washing with an isotonic solution, and advance to hypertonic as tolerated.

Benefits of Isotonic Solution
  * Easily tolerated
  * Makes an excellent maintenance nose wash

Comparison Of Hypertonic vs. Isotonic

	Hypertonic 3.0% Salinity	Isotonic 0.9% Salinity
Mucus	Jelly-like and sticky to thin and watery	No change
Membranes	Shrinks swelling	No change
Debris	Removes	Removes
Cilia	Improves transit time	No change
Allergens	80% removed	Unclear
Bacteria and Virus	Inhibits multiplication and growth	No effect
Biofilm*	Cuts and removes film	No effect
Medication	Decreased	Some decrease

Biofilm is a covering, a film, often stuck to the membranes much like plaque on the teeth or the slippery slime on river stones. This bacterial community consists of two major components: bacteria and the body's white cells (the cells which fight infections.) Biofilm is often stuck to the mucosal linings and is very difficult to remove. More than 99% of all bacteria live in biofilm communities. Some are beneficial, but biofilm can cause problems. Antibiotics kill or inhibit bacteria but if the bacteria are within a biofilm, the antibiotic may not necessarily reach them. Often, these films can often be physically removed by simply washing them away.

Hypotonic

Hypotonic means the salt concentration in the washing solution contains less salt than the body. Regular tap water is hypotonic. Remember *osmosis*? When the solution is less salty than the membranes, the fluid will move to the saltier side — in this case, to the inside of the membrane. Washing with a hypotonic solution can actually cause increased swelling of the nasal and sinus membranes. You may have noticed this effect if you have ever tried to rinse your nose with plain water instead of a salty solution. Washing with hypotonic solutions are not recommended.

Buffering, pH And Acidity

Okay, back to some basic chemistry. Hang in here — it's pretty simple and well worth understanding.

pH is a number that indicates levels of alkalinity and acidity. pH means 'power of hydrogen' which is a chemist's way of looking at relative acidity. In pH language, 7 is neutral; lower than that is acidic and higher than that is alkaline. You may have seen the 'pH scale' on a test strip for your swimming pool or spa. The lower the pH, the more acidic your pool water is. Higher pH means the water is alkaline. The nasal membranes have a pH of about 5.3 − 7.0, on the acid side of neutral. Typical tap water has a pH of about 6, also on the acidic side of the scale.

Now, what does **buffer** mean? A buffer is a chemical that keeps something where it should be. It prevents adverse swings. It shields, cushions and protects. And in the case of nose washing solutions, buffering adjusts and sets the pH for the most comfortable and effective washing solution. If the solution is alkaline, with a higher pH, the high salt content is more easily tolerated by the mucous membranes. If one washes with a very salty solution but one devoid of buffering, it may sting.

Bicarbonate raises the pH of water (∼ 6) to a more alkaline level (7.5 − 8.5) which appears to be beneficial. Bicarbonate helps soothe irritated membranes, and we are more likely to keep using a solution that feels good. Studies have shown that buffering also increases the efficiency of ciliary clearance and augments healing.

Sometimes people who are congested and irritated by inflammation find that even neutral salt may sting the raw nasal passages a bit. We do know that the saline wash actually augments healing and that this uncomfortable sensation is very temporary. Often the second or third washing will feel comfortable. Therefore, I suggest always beginning with an isotonic solution and advancing to hypertonic as tolerated. Most people can advance within three days, easily tolerating and enjoying the sensation of a cleaner nose.

Benefits of Buffered Solutions
- Higher pH with sodium bicarbonate improves mucus flow
- Augments healing of tissues
- Soothes membranes
- Increases tolerance to very salty solutions
- Increases the amount of allergens *(inflammatory mediators)* washed away.

Dr. Talbot and Dr. Parsons both have incorporated buffered hypertonic saline nasal irrigation for their patients with acute and chronic sinusitis and for those having undergone sinus surgery. In their 1997 study, the ciliary function in various saline environments was evaluated and they concluded the following: " *The outcome showed buffered hypertonic saline nasal irrigation to improve mucociliary transit times, while buffered normal saline had no such effect. Buffered hypertonic saline nasal irrigation is an important addition to the care of sinus disease".*[7]

Interesting Facts

- Normal pH of nose = 5.3 - 7.0
- Average mucus produced each day = 1 pint to 1 quart
- Typical pH of adult nasal mucus = 5.5 - 6.5
- Typical pH of infants and children nasal mucus = 5.0 - 6.7
- Best pH to foster mucus clearance 6.9 - 9.5
- Buffering is beneficial for both hypertonic and isotonic solutions

Special Section: Let's Hear From The Experts

David S. Parsons, M.D. specializes in adults and children with difficult sinus problems, and in pediatric ear, nose and throat care. He wrote and edited one of the largest selling books in the world on sinus care, and created three internationally distributed CD-ROMs describing comprehensive sinus care, emphasizing the Minimally Invasive Surgical Technique, which he helped develop.

For time longer than we know (at least three millennia), salt water has been used for nasal irrigation. When the amount of salt in a specific volume of water is the same as what is in your blood, we call it "saline." When the nose is washed with saline, we call this a "balanced solution" because the amount of salt on either side of your nasal membrane is the same. But we questioned how a balanced solution can reduce nasal swelling. So we performed tests comparing saline to "hypertonic saline," or an unbalanced solution with more salt than is in your blood.

Our findings were unexpected. Patients felt the high salt concentration was much better, but clearly stated they would not use it, because it burned the inside of their nose. Therefore, we buffered it with bicarbonate. Patients, including young children, informed us that we now offered the best solution they had ever used.

We then performed a number of studies to measure objectively the true benefits of Buffered Hypertonic Nasal Saline Irrigation. *Every study done revealed that this solution was superior to either normal saline, water, or un-buffered hypertonic saline. Finally, we tested a variety of strengths for the optimal solution and clearly showed that 3 times the amount of salt than is in your blood is best. The amount of bicarbonate was enough to raise the pH one unit (from about 6.4 to 7.4) thus creating an alkaline solution.*

Further studies by an independent lab revealed that the frequency of the beating of little cilia (hair like structures on each cell surface) increased 10 to 12 times/minute resulting in much better clearance of secretions from both the nose and the sinuses. This was most unexpected. We were only trying to keep the nose from burning but the side benefits of the bicarbonate were very impressive.

Over the years, we have received letters and emails from all over the world from happy users of this product. The patients and parents report a decreased need for emergency room visits, fewer antibiotics, few X-rays, less discomfort and a healthier state of being.

Our interest in this product was purely from a standpoint of trying to find the best care for our patients. None of our research team ever received a penny from any of the products available using this recipe. We have no financial interest in any company that produces this product. But we know that it works better than any other solution available…and so do our patients.

David S. Parsons, M.D., FAAP, FACS
Clinical Professor, Universities of North & South Carolina
Pediatric Otolaryngology, Charlotte Eye, Ear, Nose and Throat

From The Expert

Advantages Of Hypertonic Solution

Nasal washing inflamed and swollen sinuses is most effective when solutions contain high salt concentrations. Concentrated salt solutions are known to shrink swollen tissues to enhance drainage and to stop bacterial putrification (salt preserving as in salt pork). Gargling with salty water speeds a sore throat to recover. Many bacteria including Staph Aureus contain a higher salt concentration than our blood. Antibiotics that work to weaken bacterial cell walls allow water to move osmotically into bacteria to make them swell up and burst. High salt may also weaken ionic bonds by which bacteria adhere to epithelial cells.

Our own white blood cells use hydrogen peroxide to destroy many types of dangerous bacteria such as Staphylococcus aureus (SA) and methicillin resistant SA (MRSA). For MRSA skin infections, salty peroxide solutions are being recommended. Likewise, nasal washing devices can deliver diluted hydrogen peroxide as well as salt, sodium bicarbonate and antibiotics at concentrations deemed appropriate for the situation. The versatility and utility of nasal washing has been overlooked far too long.

Marilyn James-Kracke, PhD
Associate Professor of Medical Pharmacology & Physiology
Department of Medical Pharmacology & Physiology
School of Medicine, University of Missouri

Additives For Your Nose Wash Solution?

Due to the many questions I frequently receive regarding additives, I chose to include this section.

What's your preference? Some like it mild and some like it stronger. Salt solutions come in many variations and a number of people add additional ingredients to their wash, at home. The list is long, so for the purposes of this book, I am listing just a few of the possibilities. This listing is not an endorsement. I suggest you do your own investigation, ask your medical provider or if uncertain, play it safe and use a prepared solution proven to do no harm. **Use these with caution after you are well informed about their use.**

Xylitol

Xylitol is a 5-carbon sugar alcohol found in many fruits and vegetables, also produced in small amounts by the human body. It is as sweet as sugar and manufactured from birch trees in Finland, cane bagasse, and corncobs. Xylitol is a sugar which does not encourage tooth decay and because it is absorbed more slowly than table sugar, it is useful as a low-calorie alternative sweetener.

There is a suggestion by some that chewing xylitol gum may help prevent ear infections. There are two mechanisms for this; the act of chewing helps open and close the Eustachian tubes, encouraging ventilation. In addition, some report xylitol prevents the growth of bacteria in the Eustachian tubes by making it difficult for the bacteria to adhere to sugar compounds. This effect may result in fewer harmful bacteria in the nose.

Too much xylitol can become toxic. It acts as a laxative and can cause low blood sugar. Too much of anything is never good.

Hydrogen Peroxide

Some people use 3% diluted hydrogen peroxide to rinse the nasal cavities. Hydrogen peroxide (H_2O_2) is a simple molecule, really just water with one extra highly reactive oxygen atom. When hydrogen peroxide enters a bacterial cell, it uses that extra highly reactive oxygen molecule to wreak havoc, destabilizing the cell to the point of destruction. Humans are not harmed because our cells have a chemical called *catalase,* which easily breaks down hydrogen peroxide into simple water and oxygen. Bacteria lack catalase and cannot develop a resistance to hydrogen peroxide. Furthermore, dilute solutions of hydrogen peroxide are very inexpensive and available at any drug store.

Although many individuals swear it works, there is no scientific support for the effectiveness of a hydrogen peroxide wash. I would not suggest this for children or those with sensitive nasal passages.

Silver

Colloidal silver is a liquid suspension of submicroscopic particles of silver. It is known that silver has antibacterial properties but toxicity is a significant and serious concern. The usefulness of silver for nasal irrigation is controversial. Colloidal silver was used as a mainstream antibiotic prior to the 1930s and it has a long history as a disinfectant for hospitals, but this use was discontinued decades ago. Silver nitrate was applied throughout the 20th century to newborns' eyes to prevent infection. Silver sulfadiazine creams have been used in burn centers for a century and continue to be used today. Long-term use of silver preparations can lead to silver toxicity (*argyria* — the skin turns ashen-gray with silver salt deposits in the skin, eyes, and internal organs.)

Antibiotics/Antifungals

Pharmacists and doctors have begun to add antibiotics directly to nasal wash solutions, delivering the medication directly to the infected areas. Delivery directly to the infected area offers some benefits. For example, this approach reduces the body's total exposure to the antibiotics. Additionally, direct washing with antibiotics eliminates the destruction of normal intestinal balance. Finally, it may reduce the incidence of allergic reactions to antibiotics.

Aromatherapy/Essential Oils

Essential oils and herbs can be quite powerful and they should be respected for their potential to both heal and harm. Some suggest very small amounts may be helpful if included in a nasal wash solution, but one should pay special attention to all safety precautions before use.

- Keep away from children
- Remember, these are flammable
- Monitor for allergy to aromatic oils. When using for the first time, use only one drop to test for sensitivity to the oil
- Read all safety instructions
- Learn and understand each additive prior to use

To summarize: various nasal rinse combinations have been studied, including isotonic and hypertonic saline, with and without buffering, with additives such as colloidal silver, antibiotics, and herbs. Consistently, hypertonic buffered saline solution has proven to be effective for congestion from any source. Isotonic buffered saline works well for overall daily washing.

Nose Wash Style — So Many Choices! How To Choose?

Nasal irrigation can be accomplished through a variety of methods — everything from sniffing salt water from the cupped hand to the use of infant suction bulbs. These methods are not really irrigation, they are moisturization. Many more options are available today for those who are serious about daily washing. There are three general major types of irrigation:

- Gravity based systems, like the neti, allow the flow of fluid to drain into and out of the nasal and sinus cavities. There is no positive pressure. This comes with the disadvantage of less control of the fluid flow and therefore, difficulty in flushing when congested.

- Positive-pressure irrigation means that the solution is propelled into the nose. This is achieved by a syringe type device, a squeeze bottle device that propels the solution against gravity, or a squeeze bottle device that propels along with gravity. Some systems offer the user control of flow pressure.

- A motorized device designed specifically for irrigation uses both positive-pressure and pulsatile irrigation. This is very effective but can be expensive, and machines tend to be neither child friendly nor travel ready

The Importance Of Head Position

Both the wash system as well as the head and neck's position determine the direction of flushing. Some systems encourage flow along the nasal floor, in the same path as the air we breathe, while others flush upward into the sinus cavities. In addition, if you have to bend or twist your neck to create a flow, it can cause neck pain, dizziness, or a lack of control. Children and older adults are among those most susceptible to problems with head positioning.

First, I have to confess, I'm not a natural swimmer nor do I enjoy the feeling of jumping into water and flooding my head and sinuses. Ouch! How can I get my 2-year-old patients to wash regularly? It has to feel good for me, first.

I always instruct my patients to wash, as I personally prefer, with a straight neck, no bending or twisting of the neck (*neutral neck*) and head in line with the rest of the spine. When the solution flow follows the natural direction of airflow, along the nasal floor, the feeling is comfortable, with no sensation of choking or drowning. This flushing, if positive pressure is constant, sets up a negative pressure area outside of the sinus openings and results in an evacuation of the sinus cavity, encouraging mucus to drain outward. No fluid enters into the sinus cavity. (see Chapter 6)

In systems that flush upward, the solution can enter the sinus cavities. This may result in a feeling of increased head pressure. Many experts believe this upward direction of flow washes the dirt, along with solution, into the sinus cavity. Hopefully, these irritating particles will exit with the mucus when the solution drains.

The position of the head during nose washing is determined by the type of irrigation system being used. You can see a clear comparison of systems and necessary head positions in the figures below.

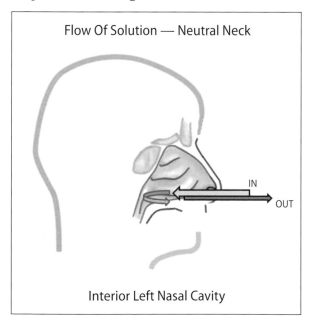

Flow Of Solution — Neutral Neck

IN

OUT

Interior Left Nasal Cavity

Flow Of Solution — Flexed Neck

IN

OUT

Flow Of Solution — Twisted And Flexed Neck

IN

OUT

Consider The Volume

Washing can be accomplished by using small amounts of water or larger irrigation flows. Imagine a dirty, congested nose. You can spray some water onto the tissues, and this may add a few droplets of moisture but it will not cleanse like a full flush with continuously flowing water.

When you are first learning to wash, use a small squirt through each nostril, just enough to have a bit of solution exit the opposite side. Often, as little as one ounce per side is adequate. If you already are an experienced nose washer, or congested or exposed to infection or pollution, two to three ounces can be used. If you suspect or have been diagnosed with an infection of the nose, sinuses, ears or asthma flare up, you may find a full four ounces is needed. Some just prefer smaller volumes, others enjoy the feeling of a continuous washing. Follow your comfort instincts and never force any fluid; it should go in easily. As you gain confidence, let comfort be your guide.

Technique And Style

First time washers should always begin with a small amount of warm washing solution and increase as your personal preference directs. Over the sink or in the shower is the best place to learn how to wash. Often a mirror can help guide you in regards to the device and head position.

If your bottle or other device has a tip that allows a complete seal against your nostril you will have a more thorough and controlled washing experience. When you are able to create a good seal, the solution is encouraged to flow out the other side of the nose, creating the most effective wash. So use your mirror to practice this part of the technique too.

Repeat the washing with the opposite nostril. Always allow the drainage to flow naturally from the nose BEFORE blowing the nose. Blow gently! Always blow gently. If one blows too forcefully, one can experience popping or pain in the ears.

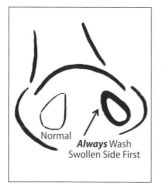

Normal

Always Wash Swollen Side First

For Moderate To Severe Congestion

If there is severe congestion on one side, begin by washing, *gently*, the congested side only! As you continue to wash with a hypertonic solution, the swollen membranes will shrink. It may require washing on the congested side several times per day for several days before the nasal passage opens enough to exit the opposite nostril. Once the fluid exits the other side, then it is safe to wash into the unplugged side. Remember, never force it.

A familiar complaint from first time nose washers is, "It tastes icky!" or "It feels funny when it goes into my throat." But an effective nasal wash technique keeps the solution flowing through the nose, and if this is done correctly none will drip down the throat. It's a learned technique but an easy one to master.

Closing off the throat while you wash is accomplished simply by using the back of your tongue to block the throat. Nose washers have various suggestions to describe their technique:

- Some say make the beginning of the "k" sound; this lifts and thickens the tongue in the back.
- Some say hold your breath; this works for me, personally.
- Some say it's the same as when they are getting their teeth cleaned at a dentist office; it's natural to close the throat in that situation.
- Others just "do it naturally." Many kids do this without even thinking about it.

If you do not master this, then you may taste some of the solution in your mouth. This is not harmful, but a bit less effective, and some people find it unpleasant. Just rinse with water and spit. Practice makes perfect.

" In One Side And Out The Other

My mom has been telling everyone she knows about washing her nose. She will ask people, "Did you know that if you close up your throat and squirt something up one side of your nose, it will run out the other side?" Then she proceeds to tell them all about the benefits of nasal washing. "

Sarah R., Miami, Florida

A Comfortable Habit

The salt concentration of the wash solution will vary depending on your comfort level, experience, and tolerance. If you experience a burning or stinging sensation, dilute the salt concentration in the solution and then increase the amount of salt as you can tolerate it. Most people increase their tolerance for higher salt concentrations with regular daily nose washing.

A comfortable habit involves a washing system that is easy to perform, feels good, has the right amount of buffered salt, and provides the best results. If you find the right system for you, you are more likely to wash regularly and reap the benefits of this daily practice.

All In One Place: Common Nose Washing Systems

Neti Pot: Most modern neti pots are made of clay, opaque plastic or stainless steel. The neti requires bending forward, flexing the neck and rotating the head, so the saline solution can be poured into one nostril. Gravity allows the solution to flow through the nasal passages and out the other nostril. The flow pressure depends on head position in addition to the position and elevation of the neti. The flow also depends upon the amount of obstruction in the nasal tissues, such as from congestion, a deviated septum or even benign growths on the turbinates (*polyps*). Neti allows the debris just inside the nose to be introduced into the sinus cavities, with the expectation that it will drain back out again. This position may also allow the solution to enter into the ear.

Squeeze Bottle: Squeeze bottles are made of plastic with a firm plastic nozzle. Using a squeeze bottle usually requires bending forward and flexing the neck, allowing the solution to be squeezed up into the nostril and sometimes into the sinuses. Flow pressure is determined by how vigorously or gently the bottle is squeezed; the flow from a squeeze bottle must work against gravity. Some squeeze bottles have a straw, some do not. Most encourage a full bottle of solution to be used for each washing. Some squeeze bottles have a bellows-type pump on the side of the bottle. Some have a 90 degree angle at the neck of the bottle, allowing the flush to travel along the nasal floor. However, these may be awkward to use, placing the bulk of the bottle in your face while you wash.

Nasopure: The bottle is made of non-leaching # 4 low-density polyethylene plastic with a closeable nozzle. The design of this bottle allows a neutral head position, with no bending forward, flexing of the neck or rotating the head. Nasopure allows solution to be flushed along the nasal floor, the same path that our air follows, then making a U-turn and exiting the opposite nostril. Gravity and the amount of pressure determine the rate of flow. Typically, a full 8-ounce bottle can last for 4-7 days. If several ounces of solution is used, one can actually feel a release, a plunging, so to speak, of the sinus and inner ear cavities without any solution entering the sinus or ear cavity.

Syringe: The tip is soft silicone and is available in several sizes. This is a positive pressure device and allows the user to point in any direction. Two hands are often required to use this system.

Pulsating Mechanical Irrigator: These electric irrigators require a period of adjustment but once the user is comfortable with this system, it is very effective in cleansing the nasal and sinus tissues. Cost and convenience have been the main hurdles reported to me by my patients.

" No More Taco Neck

The fact that I would be able to flush my nose without contracting "taco neck", and avoid the chiropractor visit was totally what I needed. I have had rhinoplasty (a nose job) to help control sinusitis and allergies to dust, mold, grass, pollen and most things green and or blooming. It was after that surgery that my ENT surgeon instructed me to use saline in order to maintain sinus health now that the cavities had, in essence, been rotor rootered.

I have been amazed at the outcome of the saline flushes. I have year around allergies, which means I spent more time sick than well. Since using the saline solution flushes I have not had any sinusitis for close to ten years. Before the surgery, I had sinusitis continually for five months and no amount of antibiotic could get rid of it. This totally changed my life. "

Al Borsella, Kansas City, KS

" All Junk Cleaned Out

I began using a nasal wash last year, it is fantastic! It cleared out major junk! It is so much easier to use than a neti pot! "

Sally K., St. Louis, Missouri

Nasal Irrigation Systems	Neti-Style Vessel	Upright Vessel
Neck Position	Bend, flex and rotate neck	Neutral head and neck
Pressure Control	Gravity	Gravity and positive pressure
Flow Control	Dependant on angle of head, elevation and position of vessel, degree of nasal blockage	Limited
Hand Grip	Some lack secure grip	Adequate
Nasal Seal	Variable	Adequate
Tip Design	Some tips can scratch nasal lining	Adequate
Sinus Draw	None	Partial
Kid Friendly	No	No
Travel Ready	No	No
Solution Level	Difficult to see	Visible
Durability	Made of clay, steel or opaque plastic	Yes
Shower Friendly	Awkward, potential for breakage if ceramic	Variable
Dishwasher Safe	Varies	Yes
Ease Of Cleaning device	Can be difficult due to narrow tip	Yes
Salt Packets	Varies. Mix your own solution	10.5 gram weight
Duration Of Salt Supply	Discard solution after 8 hours	Manufacturer recommendations vary
Salt Composition	Variable, usually non-buffered	Sodium Chloride Sodium Phosphate - Potassium Phosphate
Duration of Mixed Solution	Make fresh mixture for each nostril	8 oz per washing

NASOPURE	**Squeeze bottle with billow or straw**	**Syringe**	**Pulsatile Irrigation**
Neutral head and neck	Bend and flexed neck	Neutral or flexed neck	Neutral head and neck
Gravity and positive pressure	Positive pressure, against gravity	Positive pressure	Mechanical
User controls flow, from small squirts to continuous flushing	Adequate	Limited	Mechanical
Ergonomically comfortable	Adequate	1-2 hands	Easy
Complete seal	Adequate	Adequate	Adequate
Safe, comfortable, snaps closed	Good	Good	Good
Strong fluid flush along nasal floor, "draws" mucus and debris out of sinus cavity	None	None	None
Approved for children as young as 2 years old	Variable	Variable	No
Extremely portable; tip snaps shut to prevent leakage	Variable	Variable	No
Visible	Visibility varies with different systems	Single use	Visible
Made of #4 Low-density Polyethylene, Non-leaching	Yes	Yes	Unknown
Yes	Adequate, if premixed	Yes	No
Yes	Yes	Yes	No
Yes	Variable, straws can be difficult to clean	Unclear	N/A
3.75 gm weight	Variable, some packets less than 2 gm weight	Some products include 10 packets, each 2.5 gram wt	Packets sold separately: 33 packets - each 5 gram wt
Discard solution after 7 days	Single packet per 8 oz, single use	1 packet per use	38 packets, approximately 1 month daily use supply
2:1 sodium chloride/ sodium bicarbonate mixture	39:1 sodium chloride:sodium bicarbonate mix	99.9% purified sodium chloride	Sodium chloride, sodium bicarbonate, xylitol, potassium chloride, calcium chloride
8 oz can last up to 4-7 days	8 oz Per Washing	Filled syringe per washing	Single Use

I had seen a Neti pot before and thought them to be weird. So I found a nose wash that made sense for me. No turning the head this way and that and whatever else. It just seemed to be an easier way to wash, and easier means I KNEW my husband would be more apt to use it. We are both at full strength solution and we can both feel a difference. It is taking my husband a little more time, because his head has been clogged for 30 years. He has only taken pills if he got REALLY bad. He has never liked to take pills or vitamins, but he is all about this washing thing; he understands it. **"**

Janis P., Boston, Massachusetts

Special Section: Let's Hear From The Experts

Dr. Kelvin Walls is an Ear, Nose and Throat Specialist, a diplomat of the American Board of Otolaryngology. For almost 20 years, he has consulted on both adult and children with nose, sinus and ear woes. His unique approach to treating these problems has encouraged and empowered his patients to actively participate in their medical care. Who better to understand the beneficial effects of nasal washing than an ENT surgeon?

Direct From The Surgeon

I am putting myself out of business because of my recommendations for nasal irrigation. Increased use has mitigated my patients' nasal, ear and throat complaints as much as any new surgical technique or medical therapy. In my opinion, most otolaryngologists are very comfortable prescribing the use of irrigation after surgery. In the past I suggested the use of nasal irrigation for its effectiveness in removing dead tissue, which essentially helps clear a patient's nose after nasal and/or sinus surgery. I have found that the anxiety and stress associated with post-operative recovery can make many patients unreceptive to the trial and benefit of nasal irrigation. Therefore, I now recommend nasal washing before surgery, when they are more open and amenable to understanding and trying a treatment method that is new to them.

Almost immediately after I had begun suggesting that pre-op patients use nasal irrigation, I noticed that my patients who washed before surgery were dropping off of my surgery schedule. They stated that they were "getting over" their symptoms and their condition had dramatically improved. My first instinct was to attribute this decline in surgery numbers to the patients' reluctance to have surgery. But after a closer look into why these patients improved, I found that nasal cleansing was the key. Patients who washed before (or as it turned out, instead of) surgery were having success treating some of their symptoms for the first time ever. I now teach nasal washing as a frontline therapy for all my patients who have sinus issues.

One of the joys of encouraging the use of the irrigation is hearing the testimonies of my patients' success with nasal irrigation. After initially introducing the idea and getting reluctant attitudes about trying it, they often are pleasantly surprised at how well they respond to the treatment. It seems that the more chronic the symptoms the more benefit people get from the irrigation.

Usually, with a sense of disbelief, the patients will say, "This has changed my life. I can't believe that it took me this long to find out about this. This is the first time I have been able to go all winter and haven't got a cold. If I did get a cold, it didn't go into a sinus infection or go into my ears."

Kelvin Walls, M.D.
Otolaryngologist (Ears, Nose, Throat — Head and Neck Surgeon)
Lees Summit, Missouri

CHAPTER 6

Nasopure

Nasopure is my patented design. I want to be 100% clear, with full disclosure, that Nasopure is my baby. I am biased. But I honestly don't care whether you wash your nose with my product or something else, as long as you *wash your nose every day*!

I have been recommending nasal washing for more than 20 years, at first with neti. But my patients taught me the reasons why they didn't like washing their nose. They told me what was keeping them from washing daily, or at least at the first sign of congestion. After researching the literature and evaluating the systems available around the world it was apparent to me that it was time to develop my own system. A system even my 2-year old patients could use.

I want you to imagine, for a moment, that you have come to my office for medical care. You express concern because you have been prescribed a nasal steroid (by another practitioner) and although it is working, you now have developed nose bleeds. You also share concerns about the long terms effects as well as the cost of the steroid medication.

I review your entire medical history with you, I conduct a complete physical exam, and now we are ready to learn from each other. I review diet, environmental controls, daily hygiene habits and share that these changes, if incorporated into your life, may indeed reduce the need for the steroids. But when I propose that you wash your nose as part of daily hygiene, you reply, "You want me to do what, Doctor?!?"

Yes, I want you to wash your nose. However, I wouldn't ask you to do something so unfamiliar without providing you with the right tools or the technique to use them. So this is when I begin to explain.

Most people who wash their nose for the first time assume they must tilt their head up or down or twist it. NO. With Nasopure, you keep your head straight, keeping your neck in line with the rest of your spine. I have noticed, personally and by listening to my patients, that when washing with an upright head position, one does NOT experience the uncomfortable sensation of drowning, head filled with water, or any pressure. The goal is to have an enjoyable and satisfying experience, not an uncomfortable one. And nose washing, when done correctly, feels soothing and refreshing, as it should.

There is a technique to using the Nasopure bottle, a technique backed up by scientific principles. If you follow the instructions carefully and apply just a bit of practice, you will soon be enjoying your nose washes like a pro.

The Nasopure Effect

virus
debris
mucus
irritants
bacteria
pollen

Some wash systems claim to wash out your sinuses. However, the Nasopure system washes your nose, and in doing so, encourages your sinuses to drain naturally. This is what I termed the *Nasopure Effect.* Successfully washing the nose, clearing the tiny cilia so they can sweep effectively again, and using a law of physics called Bernoulli's Principle creates the most complete daily wash possible.

This is how it works: Have you ever noticed how a swiftly moving river draws slower streams into its flow? This is Bernoulli's Principle in action. Bernoulli noticed that as fluid flows more quickly through narrow areas, the pressure within the fluid actually decreases. The faster the flow, the lower the pressure. This lower pressure acts as a suction. This is why we see small streams pulled into the swiftly moving flow of large rivers.

Imagine that your nose, with Nasopure flowing through it is the river you create each time you wash. Your sinuses are stagnant ponds with small outlets allowing them to drain into the nose. When the saline solution flows past these sinus outlets, the flush has a lower pressure as compared to the pressure in your sinuses. The pressure difference is what draws out the contents of the sinus cavities just like a swiftly moving river would drain a small pond. At a minimum, the sinus outlets are opened by cleansing and shrinking any swelling, allowing those sinuses to drain naturally. In addition, YOU control the speed of flow, so you control the pressure differential.

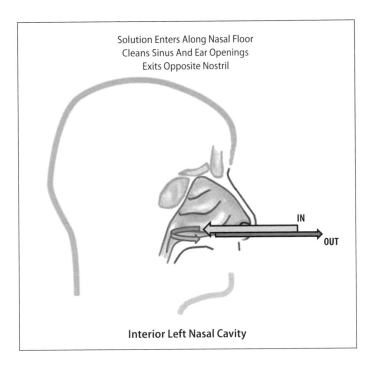

Solution Enters Along Nasal Floor
Cleans Sinus And Ear Openings
Exits Opposite Nostril

IN

OUT

Interior Left Nasal Cavity

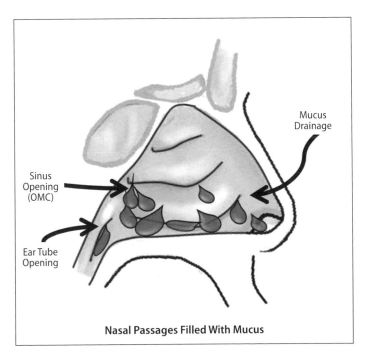

Mucus
Drainage

Sinus
Opening
(OMC)

Ear Tube
Opening

Nasal Passages Filled With Mucus

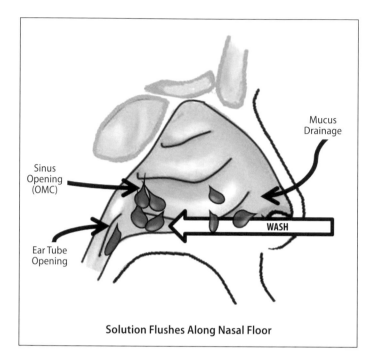

Mucus Drainage

Sinus Opening (OMC)

Ear Tube Opening

WASH

Solution Flushes Along Nasal Floor

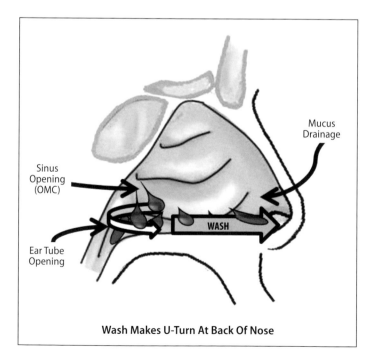

Mucus Drainage

Sinus Opening (OMC)

Ear Tube Opening

WASH

Wash Makes U-Turn At Back Of Nose

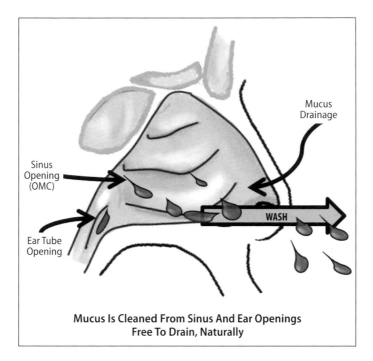

Mucus Is Cleaned From Sinus And Ear Openings
Free To Drain, Naturally

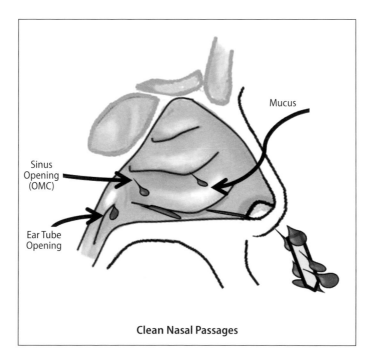

Clean Nasal Passages

When sinuses and ears are inflamed, I suggest a gentle squeeze on your bottle so you do not irritate those tender tissues. When they are not inflamed, you may want to create a more rapidly moving stream of saline that will be more aggressive in drawing out the sinuses' contents. In this way, you will be more likely to maintain clean and open passages, thus avoiding infections. You have control.

But for Bernoulli's Principle to work in cleaning out your nose and sinuses you need to direct the flow of solution across the floor of the nasal cavity so it can flow past the sinus openings, creating the pressure differential that drains the sinus contents. If you shoot your solution up instead of back then you may be aiming directly at the openings to the sinuses. This is like diverting your river directly into the pond's outlet — a situation that not only blocks the outward flow, but also can cause fleeting discomfort as pressure is forced into tiny and closed spaces. That is exactly why the Nasopure design works; its direction and flow is distinctive. Because the flow follows the natural path of air intake, the user does not get the sensation of drowning. It feels comfortable.

So read the instructions, practice your technique, and visualize a swiftly moving river of pure saline flowing past the sinus ponds, drawing out their contents and releasing them as the river flows along the floor of the nose. Finally, take a deep breath, and enjoy the sensation of a clear nose and open sinuses. So good! Thank you, Mr. Bernoulli.

A mention about the salt components in Nasopure. These are pharmaceutical grade, fine granules of sodium chloride and sodium bicarbonate combined in a ratio, which is scientifically supported to be the most effective and comfortable. The buffering added by the inclusion of the sodium bicarbonate can augment healing of tissues. This mixture is free of trace minerals and due to the tiny granule size, it dissolves instantly and is soothing to the membranes.

After many of my patients were using the Nasopure system, I decided I wanted to document their objective responses to using this device so I designed a formal study. This study was approved by the University Of Missouri Investigational Review Board in 2004. This board's function is to ensure that all approved medical studies are both safe and scientific. Regular Nasopure users responded to questions retrospectively (after they washed regularly for a minimum of one month). The results confirmed what other studies report. Overall, patients reported that their symptoms were improved or eliminated and that their medication use was reduced. Overall satisfaction was clearly demonstrated.

Detailed Instructions For Using The Nasopure System

Sophie, age 7

Washing your nose with any nasal irrigation system is most effective when done correctly. So, please read the detailed, step-by-step instructions with any system you choose to use. I suggest following my instructions and allowing three days to perfect the technique, although many people feel the results immediately. It may take practice.

It is interesting to note that most children can learn this technique almost immediately while adults may need to get over past experiences with other systems. Specific instructions for teaching children how to wash their nose can be found in Chapter 7.

The best time to incorporate washing into your daily routine is in the shower, or during dental hygiene, while leaning over a sink. The key is to integrate the habit.

Preparing Your Solution

1. Always begin the week with a clean bottle and tip. You can wash your bottle with soapy water, making sure to rinse it well.

2. Fill the bottle with water. If you can drink the water, you can use it for making your solution. Most prefer to use warm water but others use water at room temperature.

3. Add the salt packets as desired, gently mix. Make an isotonic solution for beginners or if you prefer the milder mix. A hypertonic solution is best for congestion, infection, or after exposure. *See Solution Guide.*

Using Nasopure

4. Pull the tip open and place the bottle tip into one nostril creating a good seal. Keep your head straight and look forward. You may want to lean your upper body forward from the hips so the draining water doesn't run down your chin. Point the bottle tip toward the back of the throat with the bottom of the bottle elevated. DO NOT point the tip upward. (see figure 85). Make certain the water level is horizontal to

the floor; the bottom of the bottle will almost be pointing toward the ceiling.

5. Seal your throat with your tongue as if you were gargling, or beginning to make a "K" sound, or just hold your breath. Some mimic what they do unconsciously while having their teeth cleaned at the dentist's office.

    NOTE: Learning how to block your throat may take practice. Blocking the throat prevents the solution from reaching the mouth, preventing a salty taste. If this occurs, it is not harmful. Just rinse with plain water.

6. **Gently squeeze the bottle,** allowing solution to wash along the nasal floor and exit the opposite nostril.

    At first, squeeze just a small amount of solution, enough to exit the opposite nostril. Once you are comfortable with the technique you can squeeze for a longer time, flushing a larger volume through. Larger volumes are helpful for congestion, infection, or after exposure to irritants or infections. NOTE: When first washing your nose, you may experience a slight burning sensation. This is normal and will diminish after repeated use. You can also dilute your salt concentration by adding a small amount of water.

7. Switch nostrils and repeat.

8. **Allow your nose to drain freely for a few moments, then gently blow.** If ear popping occurs, blow more gently or simply allow the solution to drain out naturally.

9. To allow any trapped solution to drain, bend forward at the waist and gently and slowly rotate your head from side to side.

10. Never force the flow. Let me repeat that: **NEVER FORCE!**

11. If your nasal cavity is **completely blocked** on one side, follow these instructions:

    Begin with an isotonic solution but advance to hypertonic as soon it is comfortable because hypertonic will actually shrink the swollen membranes. For example, if the left side is blocked, wash gently on the left side ONLY, not expecting the flush to exit the opposite nostril. Repeat 2-4 times per day. If the blockage begins to open and the solution exits the right side, then it is safe to begin flushing each nostril.

For Young Children

If your child has recurrent ear or sinus problems, is disabled, or has difficulty tolerating the wash, consult your doctor. Always have the child maintain an upright sitting position to prevent choking. Allow the child to help as much as appropriate for his or her age. Please refer to the **How To Teach Children to Wash** sections in chapter 7. Remember to always begin with an isotonic solution and use the smaller bottle. Have the child sit on an adult lap or straight-backed chair, leaning forward, bending at the waist, and facing straight ahead. If the child is old enough, have them try nasal washing in the tub, shower or over the sink. Begin by allowing the child to gently squeeze a tiny amount of solution into one nostril, assisting in directing the flush along the nasal floor. Make sure the bottle tip is not pointed upward for the most comfortable wash. Wait a few minutes before switching sides. Have the child gently blow their nose. If the child is too young to blow, gently suction the nostrils with a small bulb syringe.

How Often Should You Wash?

- Once per day at a minimum for prevention.
- Twice per day if any symptoms are present.
- Three to four times per day if infection is present.
- Wash immediately after potential exposure to airborne illness or any irritants.

Solution Guide		
Bottle Size	Isotonic	Hypertonic
4 oz.	½ swish stix	1 swish stix
8 oz.	1 swish stix	2 swish stix

Anyone can learn how to wash his or her nose. Of course, there are challenges. One, you have to incorporate the process into your daily hygiene routine, much like brushing your teeth. Another downside is that the process is not attractive or sexy, but then neither is brushing your teeth! The process is so simple and the cost so affordable, some people assume washing can't be as effective as a pill.

" Avoiding The Pain

I saw an ear, nose and throat specialist to understand why my head was always congested, in spite of taking decongestants and steroid nasal and asthma medications. An MRI showed that my sinuses to be completely clogged, so he wanted to wash them out by sticking a syringe through the bony tissue in my nose. In the meantime, I began nasal rinsing. When the doctor washed out my left sinus, nothing came out. It had already been cleared by using Nasopure, so he didn't have to do the right one. "

Fred Miller, San Carlos, California

" Clean Nose Kid

I read about Nasopure in Parents Magazine. It sounded like the perfect thing for my 5 year old son who has been having a really rough time with his runny nose due to allergies. After about 4-5 days I noticed that his nose was much more clear! I would and will definitely recommend this! Thank you guys very much! "

Jessica Capretta, Napoleon, Ohio

Possible Side Effects Of Nasal Washing

1. Burning sensation
   - Often related to mucosal inflammation
   - Will subside with continued washing
   - Will be less likely to occur if the salinity is increased only as it is tolerated

84

2. Ear popping
   - Technique: be sure to point the solution towards the back of the throat. If congested, the shrinking of the swollen ear opening allows air to percolate upward, hence 'ear popping'. This is a good sign because it means the Eustachian tube is opening up. The ear popping will subside with subsequent washings.
   - Following washing: Do Not Blow Vigorously, Never. This can cause air to be forced backwards into the ear tube.
   - Eustachian tube dysfunction already exists: if the ear already contains fluid, ear popping will occur. Just keep washing gently and this will be resolved as the Eustachian tube becomes clear.
   - Forceful washing can cause a transient popping of the ears.

3. Water drips unexpectedly from the nose after washing
   - Technique: the solution is directed upward into the sinuses where it can become trapped, unexpectedly flowing out later when the sinus ostia decongest and open. Maintain the bottle as directed, bottom of bottle almost pointing toward the ceiling, tip pointed straight back, at the level of the ear lobe, ensuring the flush along the nasal floor.
   - Swollen mucous membranes: The solution finds a hidden pocket in the swollen membrane and gets trapped. The saline decongests the nose, shrinking the swollen membranes and the leftover solution drains out. This will also be resolved once the tissues heal.
   - Too much solution is used: when a full bottle is used rather than smaller amounts of solution. This is true for only a few people.
   - Salt contents: using too little salt can cause the tissues to swell, and over time the excess water can drain.
   - Advice: if this is a problem for you, try this technique. After washing, and after allowing the natural drainage to exit from your nostrils, blow very gently. Then, slowly, bend from your waist, and allow your arms to dangle freely, relaxing there for a moment. Then, very slowly and gently turn your head so that your chin approaches or touches your shoulder. Repeat for other side. This will allow any trapped solution to drain naturally.

Important Considerations

- *NEVER block the opposite nostril to prevent solution from draining freely.*
- Do not use immediately before bed, as water may drip from your nose for several minutes after washing.
- If you experience burning or stinging, reduce the strength of the saline solution.
- Never force anyone else to wash.
- Do not lie down while using any nasal irrigation system.
- Do not microwave plastic bottles, ever.
- Wash the nose prior to using prescribed nasal sprays.
- Be gentle.
- Blow very gently after allowing the solution to drain naturally.
- Each bottle is intended for a single user, like a toothbrush.
- Discard solution after one week and remix a fresh batch after washing the bottle and cap. Rinse the cap after each use.
- Use warm solution to wash with. Cold solution can be uncomfortable. Never use hot water.
- Store solution at room temperature.
- Check out www.nasopure.com for more information or contact me for questions regarding your nasal washing experience.
- Consult your doctor if symptoms worsen or if you have a significant medical condition.

My Personal Clinical Pearls

- Any washing is better than no washing.
- Learning curves vary, so be patient.
- Kids learn easier if at least one parent demonstrates.
- Washing should always precede any prescription nasal medication.
- It usually takes 1-3 days to master the art of nasal washing.
- Always begin with isotonic and increase the salinity as tolerated.
- Hypertonic works best.
- Tongue placement is important (i.e. 'K' sound closes the throat).
- Seniors appreciate the art of nose washing.

- Never force anyone to wash.
- Water quality — if one can drink the water, one can use the water for nasal irrigation.
- If one can stand and brush their own teeth, one can learn how to wash.
- Nose washing is not sexy.
- Your nose feels refreshed and soothed after washing.
- Washing your nose represents a long-term hygiene strategy aimed at prevention.

Special Section: Let's Hear From The Experts, In This Case: Parents!

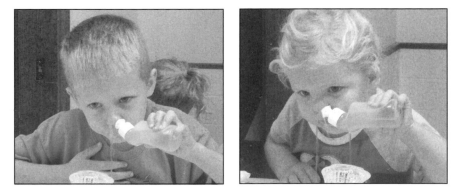

My Nasopure story began several years ago. I had heard of nasal irrigation from a couple of sources but did not know of any easy way to accomplish rinsing your nose with a "salty" solution. My introduction to nose washing was very informal, probably during a visit to our family physician during the cold and flu season. At that time I was a little apprehensive about how to correctly irrigate my nasal passages. However, I mixed up the solution as the doctors had instructed and took a stab, or rather a squirt, at "hosing my nose". To my amazement, I got it right on my first try. Didn't cough, didn't drown and I was overwhelmed with a sense of cleansing in my nasal passages. From that point forward, I was sold.

Since that time, I have had a few colds, sinus infections and such, but washing my nose has lessened or eliminated symptoms, and in general, has helped reduce the duration of my nasal related issues. As my wife and I have discovered, one of the best ways to learn and perfect the technique is to use a mirror when doing it. The visual feedback you get from the mirror will guide you on how much pressure to exert on squeezing the bottle when irrigating your nose. Another thing that we've also discovered is that doing it in the shower helps too.

Our first born child, Matthew, has experienced allergic type symptoms to common indoor and outdoor allergens (ie, dust, pollen, grasses). Fairly early in his life, around 2 years old, Matthew became a somewhat frequent user of an oral antihistamine. This medication, though improv-ing Matthew's quality of breathing, was not what we wanted for Matthew long term. When Matthew was about 3½ years old, we began introducing him slowly to washing his nose. My wife and I would demonstrate how and explain why it would clean out our noses and help us breathe better too. For Matthew, the best place for learning was in the shower. We would make a game of it see who could rinse out the best boogers first. Matthew continued to use Zyrtec on occasion as washing on a regular basis did not happen right away. But with careful persistence, Matthew became a regular washer, just like brushing his teeth daily. Now at 5½ years of age, he takes no medications for allergy related symptoms.

Matthew's younger sister Rachel, wanting to be just like big brother, took her first shot at nose washing BEFORE she was 3 years old. She saw Matthew at the sink one day with the bottle and decided she had to try it. Rachel does not suffer from allergic symptoms as severe as Matthew's but she still wanted to be like big brother. And like big brother she was. In fact she is a natural. She picked it up easier than Matthew and they both are true nose washers. I don't know if this is a coincidence, but Rachel took her first swimming lessons after learning to flush water into her nose when she was 3 and very quickly became at ease while going under water. It is my belief that learning to do hold your breath and closing off your throat has helped her advance in swimming class at a much faster pace.

One final note. Our family began using isotonic buffered salt when we started our journey. And I would certainly encourage isotonic mixture in the beginning. As we became more comfortable, we have made it all the way up to hypertonic solution. It is a little more intense, but boy does it do a thorough cleaning of your nasal passages!

I am so thankful that I have become acquainted with nasal washing. My nose and my family's noses certainly appreciate it.

Sincerely,
Michael Griffith and family
Columbia, Missouri

" Easier Than Neti

I really like my Nasopure bottle and use it routinely — especially now, in allergy and cold season. It is so much easier to use than a neti pot. I use mine in the shower, so much quicker and no mess! I am purchasing Nasopure kits for Christmas gifts. My hat goes off to you Dr. Hana for a great alternative to medicine. The swish stix are so convenient and not as harsh as sea salt. I recommend this system to people of all ages. "

Lindy Malone, Enfield, IL

" Ceramic Neti Breaks

My granddaughter has lupus, a small brain aneurysm, high blood pressure and sinus problems, so we need Nasopure to help. We recently moved and the sudden change of climate from San Francisco to Arizona's dry climate has set off her sinus problems. Then this morning she was working with her ceramic neti pot, but it broke. She called me to find out how she could get one of yours. So I looked on the bottom of my box and, God bless, your number was there. Thank you for returning my call on a Sunday and getting a Nasopure system sent so quickly. "

Jacqueline Osmer, Prescott, Arizona

Special Section: Let's Hear From The Experts

The Right Cure For Many Ills

As a rural GP and Emergency Medicine Attending Physician, I've seen the gamut of medical conditions over the past 15 years, and have explored a myriad of options for most of them. Since fortuitously stumbling upon Dr. Hana's Nasopure I've recommended it for no small variety of conditions, and have found it particularly successful in treating nasal and sinus congestion in all of its varied forms — viral coryza (head colds), allergic and irritant congestion, and both viral and bacterial sinusitis. I've certainly recommended neti pots and salt water inhalations in the past, but had found both patient acceptance and efficacy sadly problematic. The idea of pouring the contents of a tiny teapot into one's nose was a difficult sell to the non-Indian patient, and even to those who'd grown up culturally accepting such a measure! The plastic Nasopure bottle however was an object that looks more-or-less familiar to the majority of my patients, and was (rather surprisingly to me) quite readily accepted — even by young children and teenagers!

Clinically, the results have been most gratifying — with the result that something I'd initially had to "sell" somewhat to the patients has now become familiar and accepted through word-of-mouth alone in our small town! As respiratory illnesses often begin in the nose and upper airways, it's seemed to me as if "early" treatment with nose washing may actually have aborted the progression of colds in some of my patients, along with alleviating the severity of their earliest symptoms. Whether patients are suffering allergic asthma (that triggered by mold, pollens, grasses, dust mites, etc.) or irritant asthma (due to pollution, smog, chemical fumes, etc.) treatment with nasal rinsing has often provided amazing relief of both the upper airway symptoms and the secondarily-triggered asthmatic symptoms of wheeze and chest congestion. It's certainly been a life-saver for a majority of these patients, and has in many cases dramatically reduced their use of not only inhaled steroids but both short and long-acting beta agonists (i.e., salbutamol).

Not surprisingly, I've also had successes with nasal washing in treating chronic post-nasal drip, and occasionally patients have even reported a reduction in snoring as described by their sleep partners. As a practicing physician exposed on a daily basis to all manner of respiratory pathogens, I tend to practice this regimen myself near-religiously at the end of the work day to purge my nostrils of any viruses or bacteria which might be attempting to infect me. Although I've not truly documented my experience, I do feel that this intervention has served me well in helping me to avoid occupational illness despite my high-risk profession.

I would highly recommend both the daily practice of nose washing and Dr. Hana's well-designed little device to anyone with the above-mentioned conditions, or anyone with an interest in nasal health. I strongly feel that it should be a mainstay in the therapeutic repertoire of any ENT physician, pediatrician, or general practitioner.

Lawrence W. Klein, M.D.
Family Practice, Emergency, Integrative & Nutritional Medicine
Squamish, British Columbia, Canada

CHAPTER 7

Children

Kids And Colds —
The Seemingly Endless Connection

Kids get colds. On average, kids get anywhere from three to nine colds each year, depending on their age, the number of siblings in the home, and their social interactions. While these viral infections are helpful because they build immunities, in children younger than preschool age colds can lead to complications such as ear, chest and sinus infections. There are ways to minimize the number of sick days and the miseries of the cold and flu season.

The U.S. Food and Drug Administration frequently updates their advisory stating that over-the-counter (OTC) cough and cold medicines should not be given to infants and children. The cut off age for safe use of OTC medications has been revised more than once, so prudent caution is wise. Side effects of these products and the risk of overdoses are serious concerns. Washing the nose, a more holistic alternative, has few, minor side effects *and* does not contribute to the growing problem of antibiotic resistance.

Several recent studies involving children support both my clinical experience and what other doctors already know. Nasal washing in children reduces the number of colds and other respiratory infections. Those who irrigate with saline use fewer medications, including fever reducers, decongestants and antibiotics. The nasal wash groups also face shorter illnesses and fewer missed school days. This news finally supports a common sense approach I have valued since the early days of my medical practice: "If it's dirty, wash it!"

Children And Ears

Americans spend billions of dollars each year treating ear problems in children; much of it on doctor visits, drugs and surgery. Ear infections are the number one reason children visit a doctor's office, and the number of children coming in with ear infections has risen over the past decade. There are several reasons for this including bottle-feeding, increased allergies, greater pollution, more children in daycare, and exposure to cigarette smoke. Interestingly, boys develop infections in the ears more often than girls do, and it is not clear why.

Children in general seem to experience far more ear infections then adults, and this is because their Eustachian tubes are immature. (Chapter 6, Figure 33). Infants and children have a more horizontal Eustachian tube without gravity to assist in drainage. It is also much shorter and collapses more easily compared to an adult tube; the opening in the throat is more rounded, making it easier for secretions to find their way up into the middle ear. Additionally, babies tend not to swallow when they are asleep (they drool), and less swallowing means less ventilation of the middle ear. All of these differences result in a buildup of negative pressure which causes pain and this leads to restless nights.

Anyone who has had difficulty clearing their ears after flying in an airplane, or anyone who has had the congestion of a cold that "clogged" their ears knows how Eustachian tube dysfunction feels. Children with chronic nasal congestion can feel this way all the time. These children think the world always sounds muffled and it is no surprise that they cannot speak clearly. The most common causes of Eustachian tube dysfunction are allergies and respiratory infections. Traditionally doctors have given antihistamines to dry up secretions and decongestants to clear the passages. However, the side effects of these two medications can be problematic, especially in children.

Molly was brought into my clinic by her mother because the kindergarten teacher was concerned that Molly was not paying attention in class. A quick screen in the office indicated a "conductive hearing loss". Mom wanted to avoid medications if possible, so she agreed to try nasal rinsing. Soon Molly was "washing" like a pro, and two weeks later the repeat hearing test was normal. A simple and safe approach resolved her problem.

Hearing is one of the most important windows to a child's world. Through good hearing, a child learns language skills and an appreciation for the world around him or her. If you are concerned about your child's ability to hear well, speak to your physician. If the problem is chronic congestion or infections, ask about nasal rinsing. It could change your child's life.

Adenoids and tonsils are lymph tissues that normally enlarge as a child ages, peaking in size during elementary school years and beginning to shrink just before puberty. The adenoids are situated in the upper throat, in the back part of the nose, right next to the Eustachian tube opening. The tonsils are lower in the throat. These tissues will remain enlarged if constantly irritated, aggravated and stimulated by recurrent infections or allergies. These chronically enlarged tissues prevent the Eustachian tube's normal drainage, which can contribute to recurrent ear infections.

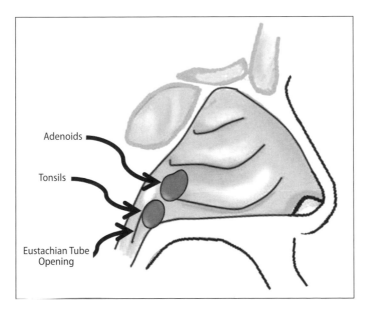

For years, doctors would automatically prescribe antibiotics when any fluid was found in the middle ear, especially in children. If the fluid persisted, they would recommend surgical placement of drainage ports, *PE tubes*, in the eardrum — a manmade exit for the fluid. These tubes do not correct the original problem, but they do allow the fluid to drain out the ear canal if the Eustachian tube is blocked. More recently, the Academy of Pediatrics acknowledged that routine antibiotics and PE tubes may not be the best approach and has now released new recommendations. A watch and wait approach to most ear infections is the newest guideline, but as in the past, it is up to each physician to decide on the necessity of using antibiotics.

These recommendations will hopefully contribute to a decrease in the overuse of antibiotics and a reduction in bacterial resistance. Using fewer medications will reduce the development of adverse drug reactions as well. Sometimes these medications are warranted, but I recommend a first line treatment that is much safer and often more effective in addressing the core issue as compared to medication: Nasal washing with hypertonic buffered salt water.

Mucus Is Free To Drain

PE Tube

Mucus Fills Eustachian Tube

From The Expert

Antibiotic overuse is a particular concern. Many children with nasal disease seem to become "antibiotic-dependent," that is, their symptoms seem to be relieved while taking antibiotics, but then relapse shortly after the treatment course ends. A new antibiotic is then started, and the cycle then repeats itself over and over, sometimes for many months.

Michael Cooperstock, M.D., MPH
Division Chief, Pediatric Infectious Disease,
Immunology, & Rheumatology
Professor of Infectious Disease
Department of Child Health
School of Medicine, University of Missouri

Tips To Reduce Ear Infections

- Breastfeed instead of bottle-feed.
- Avoid exposing your child to cigarette smoke.
- Prevent allergies, adjust living environment for fewer allergens.
- Provide healthy unprocessed foods for fewer allergies.
- Avoid daycare if your child is younger than 2 years old.
- Keep the nose clean.
- Avoid medications that dry and thicken the mucus, such as antihistamines.
- Maintain hydration, avoiding sugary juices (teach your children to drink water).
- Treat GERD (*Gastroesophageal Reflux*) if it is present.
- Apply warmed moist compresses to the outer ear for 20 minutes every few hours.
- Work with your child's medical provider so that your collaborative efforts will bring about the most effective and least invasive solutions
- If your child is getting worse, see your medical provider!

New Baby Nose

Newborns are obligated to breathe through the nose, a perfect design that reserves the mouth for breastfeeding. Their nasal passages are tiny and can easily become congested due to gastric reflux, colds, or even mild irritation. Eating becomes an issue when the infant is congested, hence the blue bulb suction which parents know all too well.

I suggest beginning with a few drops of isotonic saline, gently inserted into each nostril while the infant is sitting upright. (Babies may fret at this because they do not appreciate the salty taste, but it is not irritating to their nose.) After waiting 1-2 minutes, lay the infant down and squeeze all the air out of the blue bulb. Gently ensure a complete seal between the infant's nose and the bulb tip, and then release the pressure on the bulb. Aim the tip directly back towards the ear lobe, not upward toward the eye or toward the septum since both of these directions may cause a scratch inside the infant's tender nose. The bulb will suction the loosened mucus. Do this only once on each side. Repeat prior to each breastfeeding session and each nap if congestion continues.

School Days

When school starts at the end of each summer parents may be relieved to have their kids back in the classroom; they are also aware that this is when everyone starts getting sick again. Schools are wonderful breeding grounds for viruses and some of this illness is inevitable, even desirable. After all, fighting viruses is how we build immunities, so some illness is actually good for our health. But try to tell that to a sick kid, or the mother of a sick kid! Taking measures to prevent sickness is always a good idea, and there is much you can do to keep your kids healthy through the fall and winter months.

Teaching children to wash their hands is probably the most popular health measure. Try to reinforce this healthy habit by asking your kids to clean their hands regularly when you are with them. Make sure they wash before eating any food, even snacks. While you are teaching your children to wash their hands, it's a good idea to teach them to wash their nose also. Our grandmothers knew the health values of salt water and recently we have grown to appreciate their wisdom. Learning to wash can be fun for kids, especially when they are healthy.

When a child develops cold symptoms, I encourage parents to manage that cold with twice a day nasal washing; it is a natural decongestant and soothes inflamed mucous membranes. There are NO side effects to the simple combination of rest, fluids, washing the virus particles out of the nose and patiently allowing the body to heal itself.

Before we get into the nuts & bolts of keeping your kids' noses clean and clear, here are some very important things to keep in mind:

- Many children can prevent or reduce chronic nasal/sinus problems by regular nasal washing.
- It can be challenging to get a child to do healthful habits.
- Do not expect daily use.
- The goal is for children to become skillful and comfortable in washing.
- Use as needed to avoid illness after exposure to those who may be ill or as daily prevention for chronic symptoms.
- Children are more likely to use a formula that is free of additives because it does not burn.
- Use a child-sized bottle.
- Use a solution, either isotonic or hypertonic, that does not burn.
- Offer the child complete control.

From The Expert

I have confidence when I recommend nasal wash for my patients. With all the ear, nose and throat issues that children experience, I am certain that simply washing the nasal lining has great benefits without risk. My patients quickly learn the simple technique and I find that they use fewer medications, experience both fewer symptoms and fewer infections. Nasal washing has proven to be tolerable, safe, convenient and effective for my pediatric patients. Maintenance of nasal and sinus health with the modernized version of an ancient technique of nasal irrigation just makes sense.

Marcella R. Bothwell, M.D.
Pediatric Otolaryngology
San Diego, California

Teaching Your Child To Wash

A patient I cared for some time ago, four-year old Brianna, had ongoing ear and sinus problems and would often require multiple medications to control her allergy symptoms. I introduced Brianna to washing her nose by encouraging her to fill the bottle with warm water and just play with it during her daily bath. This helped her get the feel of the pressure needed to spray water out the tip. Both her mom and I would applaud her efforts. Next, we suggested to her that if she tried to squirt just a bit of water in her nose, it would help her blow her nose clean. Again, we applauded all of her efforts. The next step was to play a game and ask if she could make the water come out of the other nostril. Over a short period, Brianna became an expert at washing her nose without any help from her mother. Brianna's office visits and medication use decreased as she perfected her nasal washing technique.

Four-year old Sophie had similar problems. In addition, her speech development was delayed because of recurrent ear problems which stemmed from her allergies. Of course, we looked at environmental factors and her parents did as much as they reasonably could in this regard. Sophie slowly learned to use a nasal rinse much like Brianna. Only one year later, Sophie's parents have told me that she will sometimes wake up with a stuffy nose and ask to wash. Then she steps up to the sink, washes her nose completely on her own, blows, grunts like an old man and walks away saying "Now that feels good. I can breathe." At seven years young, Sophie is now a pro at nasal irrigation and she gladly demonstrates her technique to any camera or person who is interested. Most importantly, she has been free of allergy medications for years.

The overall approach to teach a child how to wash must be geared towards the child's developmental age as well as his or her past experiences. One slow step at a time, no forcing allowed. Only gentle encouragement, bribing, demonstrating and lots of positives for any success at all.

What If Your Preschool Child
Is Scared Of Water?

I have often heard a mother say, "My child is terrified of water and you want me to put water up his nose?"

First we must understand that survival is a basic instinct, so it is not just oppositional behavior that makes a child scream, flail and panic at the perception that he may become a potential drowning victim. He may have been frightened from a past experience and now has a negative memory to erase.

If you've been trying to force your child to calmly accept your attempt to squirt water in his face as a solution to a stuffy nose, forget it; you've already lost that game. So first, sit back, relax, and take a deep cleansing breath. Today we start over.

Begin by allowing your child to stand on the bath mat in a couple of inches of water, bathing his toys and toes slowly and gently. You may want to run warm water into the tub and turn off the water before you even take him in the bathroom. The loud sound of water running can be frightening to some sensitive children.

Assure him that from now on he may just stand in the tub while you wipe him down with a wet cloth. That's all. New rules. Give him control and he will amaze you.

Put some tub toys to float in the water. Over a matter of weeks, slowly raise the depth of the water to his mid shin. If you make no threats, odds are the floating toys will garner enough interest that he will begin to explore them.

Slowly now, when washing him, begin to drizzle a bit of water on his skin playfully, from the tip of the washcloth. See if you get away with it. If so, over the week ahead, drizzle a bit more. The idea is to slowly desensitize him until he is used to having water touching him, splashing on him, eventually in his face, without it setting off a panic attack.

Your child will begin to reach for the bath toys, squat to float them on the water, perhaps eventually sit. Add a doll, boats, even a nasal wash bottle — whatever will pull in your child's interest.

Once you have your child sitting in the shallow water at play, *don't say anything about it*. Treat it as a non-event. NEVER, NEVER say, "See, there is nothing to be afraid of." That simply reminds the child of his fear, and makes him begin to worry again that maybe he was right. Remember, there is no big rush. If you can manage to turn this around and instill a lack of fear, and teach him how to wash in general, he will eventually learn to wash his nose. Once a child has developed a fearful response, remember: it will take many safe, pleasurable experiences to replace those original memories, so patience is of the essence.

Understand this will take time but teaching hypersensitive children appropriate water conduct will pay off in many ways down the road.

The secret to teaching children how to wash their nose is a slow introduction, giving the child all of the control, praising them frequently for little steps and asking them to demonstrate their technique for others.

How To Teach Your 2-3 Year Old Toddler To Wash

 It can be difficult to get toddlers to do *anything* they think is suspect, so you may have a challenge ahead of you. But the effort is worth it. My best advice is to proceed slowly, be resolved to succeed, and always remember that children learn best by playing, doing and imitating what you do. Teaching a toddler to wash her nose is much like the way you teach a two year old to brush her teeth: one step at a time, no forcing, no pressure, no trauma — only fun and rewards and repeated demonstrations of good technique. You improve the technique one step at a time.

Begin by feeling comfortable washing your own nose, so that your child will see and feel your comfort level.

Next, allow plenty of bathtub play involving a nasal wash bottle. Not only does this attach a "non-medical" feel to the bottle, it allows your child to gain familiarity with the sensation of holding and squirting the bottle. Play "squirty" games with your child and a bathtub doll. Suggest, "Let's wash her tummy — squirt! Let's wash her ears — squirt! Let's wash her knees — squirt! Let's wash her nose — squirt!" Make this game a nightly routine.

Once your child is comfortable using the bottle, begin the game using your child's knees, tummy, toes, and squirt gently. Do this for several nights — maybe even a week. It is a game to the child, so allow it to be fun and unhurried. Slowly and *gently* add your child's face parts to your squirty games as you continue to squirt the dolls — cheeks, lips, outer nose — don't forget to giggle and laugh with your child, and be sure to avoid the eyes. Be very matter of fact and make it a natural part of the game. Say "*This is fun!*" Do not say, "See, that doesn't hurt!" It will not occur to your child that it *might* hurt, unless you plant the idea.

After your child is comfortable having water in her face, she may want to wipe it off with a wash cloth each time she is squirted, and that's okay too. It is time to start washing the inside of her nose. Begin with a mild saline solution and a full bottle of warm water. The solution temperature should be the same as the bath water temperature. Keep playing the same games — squirt the baby doll, squirt your child's belly button, ears, etc. Then say, "Let's wash inside your nose a little, too," and ask her to place the tip near her nose and squeeze. She may need a bit of guidance with your hand to make sure the bottle is held correctly but allow her to have all the control. Don't squeeze the bottle for her. Move right on and say, "Let's wash your big toe — squirt!" Giggle! "Let's wash your belly button — squirt!" Giggle! "Let's wash your OTHER nose — squirt!" Giggle!

The idea is to keep moving, keep your child distracted and keep it a game. If your child backs away, go back to the point of comfort in the squirty games for several days. Once she is calm and playful, begin advancing the process again, but slower. Allow your child to have control by letting her squirt you a lot more. Eventually move back to her ears, nose, forehead, etc.

Realize that for naturally fearful children this process may take weeks of "two steps forward, one step back" progress. Do not become discouraged, but remain upbeat and playful, and DO NOT allow, "See, this doesn't hurt!" to creep into your murmurs, regardless of how tempting it becomes.

If the fear of being squirted turns bath time into a huge struggle, you may want to separate washing the nose from bath time altogether, and treat it more like tooth brushing. However you go about it, it is important to allow game-playing, rewards, clapping and positive reinforcement to rule *your* behavior. Allow your child as much autonomy as possible — which may be choosing which doll, the color towel to dry off with, or the sticker she is going to put on her chart — because this will decrease the struggles you encounter. It may take some trial and error on your part — like much of parenting.

Special Section: Let's Hear From The Experts

The images below are the x-rays of a 35-month old boy who had almost continuous purulent rhinorrhea (thick runny nose) and cough over a two year period. He attends a preschool with 19 other children. He frequently experienced fevers, requiring many courses of antibiotics, and typically had relapses within the first 6 days off antibiotics. This pattern continued despite having an adenoidectomy (removal of the adenoids) four months earlier.

The view on the left shows cloudy maxillary (below the eyes) and ethmoid (between the eyes) sinuses, with only a small amount of air in the left maxillary sinus (arrow).

A dose of 23-valent pneumococcal vaccine was given, and twice-daily hypertonic buffered nasal saline irrigation prescribed. (Yes, a 35 month old child did have twice daily nasal washes!)

He returned 21 days later with no interim flare, 6 weeks since his last antibiotics, having only mild residual rhinorrhea and occasional cough. An x-ray (right), showed marked clearing of both maxillary sinuses. The ethmoid sinuses remained opacified but improved.

During the interim he had received every dose of the prescribed nasal saline irrigation, with no other medications. *Responses to the pneumococcal vaccine were excellent.*

Michael Cooperstock, M.D., MPH
Division Chief, Pediatric Infectious Disease,
Immunology, & Rheumatology
Professor of Infectious Disease
Department of Child Health
School of Medicine, University of Missouri

The view on the left shows cloudy maxillary (below the eyes) and ethmoid (between the eyes) sinuses prior to nasal irrigation. The x-ray on the right, taken 3 weeks after daily nasal washing showsmarked clearng (less cloudy) of both maxillary sinuses. The ethmoids remained opacified but improved.

How To Teach Your 4-6 Year Old To Wash

"I can do it myself!" Four to six years is certainly the "I can do it myself" age — if only they could!

Just like with a toddler, begin teaching by allowing your child plenty of play time in the tub with the nasal wash bottle to acquire a familiarity with it and attach a non-medical feel to it. It is important to remember that children this age also learn by playing, by exploring and by doing. The more comfortable your child feels with the bottle, the more successful he will be in using it for saline nose washes.

Children this age especially like to have an assigned task. It is helpful to explain why it is important to get the old, thick, crusty mucus out of their nose. Try a creative, simplistic approach such as the nose being like a cave, with big booger rocks blocking the entrance. Calling the bottle a "booger blaster" adds a little element of excitement and, may help your child envision just what his task involves.

Always give your child many opportunities to watch you wash *your* nose. Any comments from you regarding, "Boy, that feels good. Now I can breathe," communicates that what you are requesting is a habit you yourself enjoy.

Starting a sticker chart encourages compliance with the daily task and rewards your child's efforts with minimal or no nagging on your part. He can earn a sticker for each day he accomplishes the task, and an additional one for doing it cheerfully, or without being asked. Make a target out of a plastic plate, with circles marked off in permanent marker, and attach it to the shower wall. Begin by having your child practice aiming the squirt bottle and hitting a bull's eye on the target during bath time each evening for a week or so to prove his aim is good enough to take on the task of nose washing by himself. This will put him into a competitive, self-empowered mood.

Once your child is comfortable playing with the bottle, make up an isotonic salt solution and have him gently squirt the solution inside his nose, with lots of praise, whooping, clapping and side-line cheering. Immediately have him climb out of the tub and put his sticker on his reward chart. It is vitally important to remember that children this age have a very short attention span and need instant feedback and reward. You will have to be consistent in your effort to train him to be consistent in his.

Nose washing can take place in the bath, the kitchen sink, or even outdoors. Experiment with your child. Play with the bottle. Make a game out of it.

How To Teach Your 7-9 Year Old To Wash

This section assumes that your child has been exposed to some water play, likes a little adventure, and is not afraid to put her face in the water. Encouraging your child to "face up" into the shower may also take away the notion that it is somehow harmful to get water in our faces, ears, eyes or nose. Blowing bubbles with the mouth or even the nose in the clean bathwater, or encouraging the shower water to fall directly onto the face may help take away any fear of water in the face. (If water in the eyes is a huge issue, consider goggles, or you may want to look back at our information about nasal washing for younger children (2-3 year olds and 4-6 year olds) for ideas that may help with your child's developmental stage.)

Then it is time to "get down to business." Kids at this age are usually very interested in bodily functions, so they're fascinated at the idea that mucus which is allowed to stand inside their nose and sinuses "transforms" into nasty stuff that needs to be cleaned out. It may help to demonstrate your technique to reassure your child that this squirt into their nose will come back out.

While being gently firm about the necessity of this activity, turn it into a game. They can understand the idea of their nose and sinuses being like a cave. Inside, it is dark and warm, with moisture dripping off the walls. The moisture collects on the floor and hardens, forming "snot-rocks," or pools of "booger juice." Boys especially like the visuals of this! If allowed to continue, this nasty stuff can clog up their cave. If they want the "air carriers" to be allowed through, they must wash out the nasty stuff and keep the passages clean of snot-rocks and booger juice. Those with a fascination for the gross can actually watch the nasty stuff wash out into a bowl or the sink! Those with weaker stomachs should close their eyes.

Girls this age may like a game of a princess, pony or a benevolent being living in the back of a cave which needs to be kept clean for access to the world beyond. Kids this age have great imaginations. If allowed to make up their own story about their cave, and the reason they must sweep it clean with a water hose every day, you will find they are much more compliant, because the story almost becomes real for them. Positive reinforcement for such compliance works better than nagging about non-compliance.

Take a deep breath, both of you will survive!

How To Teach Your Child To Blow His Or Her Nose:

Let's All Sing: Blow, Blow, Blow Your Nose. Gently Now, Don't Scream

 Teaching your toddler or preschooler how to blow his nose may have developed into your greatest challenge as a parent thus far! Don't despair. Recent studies show that 98% of all high school students can successfully blow their own nose. But seriously, we all get tired of seeing goopy-nosed little ones running around, and wish there was an easy way to teach them to just blow all that junk out, with or without our help. Alas, it is not easy. But I do have some ideas to help you help them learn.

Remember that while breathing in and out is a natural, instinctive ability, blowing in and out — either through the mouth or the nose — is a learned behavior. It is also a rather abstract idea, and while young children are good at concrete concepts, most of them flounder when it comes to abstract thinking. So, if your kid gets this quickly, consider him or her a genius!

First, let's practice blowing air through the mouth. Buy a large bottle of bubble toy and wand and teach your child to blow bubbles. Emphasize gentle pursing of the lips as well as puffing the air as you enjoy watching the bubbles form. (Be aware that the dripping bubble mix makes a slippery mess so be mindful and careful.)

An alternate game is "Paper Chase." Let your child tear up some little pieces of colored paper. On a non-carpeted floor, mark a start and finish line with masking tape, and "time" your child blowing pieces of paper from one line to the other while lying on his belly. This game is ideal just before nap time!

Once the idea of blowing through the mouth is established, then the task is to move on to blowing through the nose. Only baby elephants are born thinking that this particular skill makes any sense.

One of the best game is "Blow the Hankie." Get a tissue. Have your child take a deep breath and clamp her teeth together. Gently hold your index finger up and down across her lips as though you are telling her to shush. Hold the tissue about an inch from her face and see if she can move it by blowing the air from her nose. If she does, SHE WINS! It may help to have her gently close off one nostril and blow through just one side at a time. This seems to help some children feel the air move through their nose while keeping their mouth closed, which is the key — and the hardest concept for children to grasp.

Be prepared to provide lots of clapping and cheering and encouragement during these games, as well as reminders about keeping lips sealed shut, breathing in and out through the nose only, etc.

For adults, practicing over and over is what makes us succeed, and children are no different. The difference for children is that they learn by play, so think imaginatively and creatively with your particular child in mind.

" *A Dad's Success Story With His Three Year Old*

I have been washing for about a year and am still enjoying how clean my sinuses feel after the shower. I do have one story to share where I ended up using the nose wash with my 3 year old daughter. She was playing with play-dough one afternoon and she must have put a small piece in her nose. I tried everything I could think of to get it out and was getting worried that she might inhale too hard and get it really stuck. So I decided to rinse her nostrils out. Well, after a few moments of the fluid sitting in her nose the piece just fell out. I was so happy that I had that nose wash bottle to get that piece out of her nose. "

Charles L., Ledgewood, New Jersey

From The Expert

Rinsing Away Kids' Allergies

Hypertonic nasal saline irrigation is something that I recommend quite often to my patients. People of all ages benefit from the decongesting, bacteriostatic action that hypertonic saline provides. Dr. Hana has done something quite unique with her product. Not only does she provide the ingredients and means to do the saline wash, she has clear, concise directions for how to effectively get the job done. This is especially an issue when dealing with children. Her written directions for different age groups and video of a 4-year old washing her nose so easily are fabulous resources for patients (and parents) to utilize.

Laurie Fowler, M.D.
Fowler Allergy Clinic
Columbia, Missouri

Special Section: Let's Hear From The Experts

Irrigation, Not Operation

Good results with nasal irrigation are not limited to adults. Many children can benefit from nasal washing as well. Because of the limited treatment options to control nasal congestion, runny nose, and cough in children younger than twelve, washing becomes even more important in this age group. The FDA in October, 2008 recommended that over-the-counter cold medication not be used in children under four years of age. Additionally, the agency cautioned that these drugs may not be safe in children from two to twelve years old. To control symptoms, parents have been encouraged to return to simpler, more natural remedies, including nasal saline drops for infants and washing for older children. Many of the children have had numerous ear infections but always seem to have a runny nose and chronic congestion. When properly instructed by their doctors and coached by their parents, nose washing can successfully be used to treat nasal symptoms in children and to help decrease colds, sore throats and ear infections.

Washing helps clear nasal secretions that can lead to chronic sniffling. I have often thought that if kids could just blow their nose they could alleviate many of their upper respiratory and ear complaints. Washing is able to help clear young noses.

Chronic sniffling can lead to negative pressure in the middle ear. This negative pressure can pull tissue fluid into the middle ear causing pain and decreased hearing. Have you have ever been on airplane and not been able to clear your ears? That's the type of discomfort a child may feel when the pressure hits. No wonder they can be cranky.

In the case of "Jamie," this four-year old was working on getting his second set of ear tubes. He got his first set of tubes when he was eleven months old. They stayed in for 2½ years. Well, that's how long he went before having another infection. Before the ear surgery there were lots of sleepless nights and lots of trips to the doctor's office. The parents were concerned the cycle may be repeating itself again. Increasingly, Jamie was complaining about earaches. The parents were not sure if he had selective hearing loss or if his hearing may actually have been getting worse.

Even though the family was quick to seek consultation with an ENT (Ear, Nose & Throat specialist) after having an initial good experience with ear tubes, they were hesitant to have surgery again. They were spending more time at the lake and wanted Jamie to start swimming lessons. They were concerned about scarring in his eardrums.

Except for some allergies, Jamie was a healthy young boy. He just seemed to always have a runny nose. Try as they did, his parents were unable to teach him to blow his nose. Jamie was too busy "doing boy stuff" to care; a long sniff of his nose or wipe of his nose with his hand was fine with him. When his allergies got bad the family relied on oral antihistamines.

On exam, Jamie seemed to be a happy, healthy child. His nose was somewhat congested with a mild increase in drainage. In general, he had a good nasal airway, mostly breathing through his nose. His tonsils were not particularly enlarged.

His ears, however, were full of fluid. The retracted nature of the ear drum and the light tan color of the fluid suggested to me that he had a thick mucus effusion resulting in a blockage-type hearing loss (conductive loss) usually corrected by treating the effusion. A hearing test confirmed that he had a 25db conductive hearing loss. I explained to the parents that this was comparable to walking around with fingers in your ears.

Usually when there is hearing loss, I tend to be more aggressive in suggesting tubes. Going into the summer months, with his desire to swim and considering his history of poorly controlled nasal symptoms, I felt it was important to give him a chance at conservative management. I strongly felt that clearing up his nose would be his best chance of avoiding surgery. Drying up his nose seemed like the impossible dream to his mother, who had long complained about the constant drip.

After reviewing the options with the family, I began to suggest nasal washing. I explained how the Nasopure system was designed with the *young nose in mind. I explained the steps to success that others had followed, including parental encouragement and demonstration. Kids who see the parents washing their nose are more likely to try it. It also helps to allow the child to play with the irrigation bottle during bath time, introducing nasal washing to him over time.*

Four weeks later at his follow up visit, I was happy to hear that Jamie had mastered the irrigation technique and Mom was happy that his nose was clean. Jamie was actually asking for the irrigation because he liked having a clean nose too.

He still had fluid in his ears, but now the retraction of the eardrum was much less and there were a few air bubbles in the middle ear. The return of air to the middle ear was a certain sign we were on the right track. Over the next few weeks he was able to clear his ears and successfully avoid surgery.

Nasal washing may not always be practical in children younger than two. But it can almost always be tried in older children to either prevent surgery or to avoid the need for a 2ⁿᵈ and 3ʳᵈ set of ear tubes.

Kelvin Walls, M.D.
Otolaryngologist (Ears, Nose, Throat — Head and Neck Surgeon)
Lees Summit, Missouri

CHAPTER 8

Just For Women

Pregnancy And Hormones

Most women develop some degree of nasal congestion during their pregnancy because of *pregnancy rhinitis*, a benign, temporary but bothersome condition. It's just another way that hormones change life for women who are expecting. Swelling of the sinuses is a common symptom during pregnancy.

In addition to the fact that a pregnant woman's blood volume increases by 40%, hormones like estrogen also cause swelling of the nasal membranes and excessive mucus production. Estrogen may change the consistency of mucus, causing it to become either very thick or very thin. All of these changes can get worse as pregnancy advances, interfering with proper breathing and restful sleep.

Medications are not always a safe option but according to scientific evidence, hypertonic nasal washes can address this uncomfortable and irritating issue safely and effectively.

Regular use of warm saline irrigation helps the mom-to-be breathe easier without potentially harmful medications. Just as a daily swim is safe during pregnancy, so is washing the nose.

From The Expert

The Tide Is Turning

As a family physician of many years and a mother of five, I have seen many situations where nasal irrigation is the best medicine available. During pregnancy when the nasal mucosa (the lining inside the nose) is congested and swollen, but medications' side effects are a major concern, I often suggest saline nasal washing. Women understand and prefer this safe, gentle approach to relieve their symptoms of nasal congestion, upper respiratory infections, and allergic rhinitis. Most of the women who have tried this approach report rapid improvement in their symptoms. Pregnant woman are relieved to have a safe alternative to systemic medications during this tender time. Despite the medical support for this option of nasal cleansing, many providers still do not incorporate rinsing before medicating. I am confident the tide is turning.

Laurel Walter-Baumstark, M.D.
Board Certified Family Physician
Hermann, Missouri

" *Pregnant And Healthy*

I am 26 weeks pregnant with our first child, a son! And I believe that using nasal washing everyday has helped me keep common colds at bay. The cold that I am currently getting over now did not get very bad at all. When I started to feel sick I started washing morning and night; that, I believe, helped me from feeling like I'd been hit by a truck. I didn't need or want to take medicine to feel better! "

Janis M., Springfield, Illinois

Women And Heart Disease; Is Air Pollution A Factor?

In 2007, the New England Journal of Medicine[8] published a study involving almost 66,000 postmenopausal women. Researchers examined the association of cardiovascular events (heart problems) with long-term exposure to tiny particulate matter. They found a strong correlation, showing that exposure to fine grit in polluted air boosts the risk of heart disease in women.

It has long been known that air pollution contributes to lung and heart disease, with women perhaps more susceptible than men. This study looked at deaths as well as heart attacks, coronary disease, strokes and clogged arteries. These problems were 24% more likely with every 10-unit rise in pollution particles.

The tiny unit particles (vehicle exhaust, factory dust, soot and various chemicals) are so small that 30 bits equal the width of a strand of human hair. This is an example of a situation where nasal irrigation can remove these particles from the nose, before they can enter the lungs and cause long term damage. We can lower the pollution level in our nose while we work on lowering the pollution level in our communities.

CHAPTER 9

The Seasoned Schnozz

Much like the rest of the body, the nose experiences change as we mature. We may become wiser, but some parts do not work as well as when we were younger. With age, there is an increased likelihood of certain nasal ailments, including increasing airflow resistance: we become more congested as we age. Mature patients frequently experience an uncomfortable dry nose and recurrent crusting.

There is a natural physiological phenomenon of alternating congestion and decongestion of the nasal airways. Most people are never aware of these fluctuations. Nasal challenges in the seasoned nose are a consequence of lower intranasal air temperature and lower humidity, combined with relatively enlarged nasal cavities. This enlargement is due to involution — a shrinking away or atrophy of the nasal membranes (*mucosa*).

We need to be mindful that taking additional medications is not a wise idea, especially for more mature patients. Moisturizing and cleansing the nasal cavity can significantly improve quality of life and further increase the enjoyment of stopping to smell the roses.

Points to remember for the seasoned nose:
- Mucus is thicker and stickier due to hormonal changes.
- Medications can have negative results on mucus consistency.
- There may be a decreased ability to detect odors.
- Tissues shrink with age.
- Moisture becomes more difficult to maintain.

" Dad Learns To Wash

My 87-year old dad is flying to England and uses his nasal wash system every day. In addition to his constant cough for 30 years that he finally got rid of two years ago when I took a nasal wash device to him, just recently he has completely gotten rid of his psoriasis. In retrospect, I think the constant inflammatory process in his throat drained his body of anti-inflammatory nutrients and so one malady leads to the next and the next. By curing his sinus and throat problems, his skin had a chance to heal completely. If my dad could learn to use a nasal wash system effectively, I think just about anyone who is fairly spry could learn to do it. It certainly has made a great improvement for my dad. Whether or not the psoriasis stopped because of nasal washing is hard to prove but getting rid of a difficult problem, like a chronic throat-choking cough, can free the immune system to heal other parts of the body.

Marilyn White, St. Louis, Missouri

Special Section: Let's Hear From The Experts

Finally, Relief!

I have a patient whom I'll call Mary (not her real name). She is a middle-aged woman who has suffered with sinus problems her entire adult life. When her complaints of congestion, headaches, nasal drainage and facial pressure became severe enough she turned to over-the-counter medication, which she had used without success. When she got tired of being sick and missing work, she would go to her doctor.

Through the years, she has seen primary care physicians and specialists to help her with her sinus symptoms. She has been on many rounds of antibiotics, nasal steroid sprays and antihistamines, at times responding to treatment only to have a recurrence of her symptoms.

It was not uncommon for her to have 4-5 sinus infections per year. In addition to her sinus complaints, which included facial pressure/pain and popping in her ears, she also complained of postnasal drainage that made her "sick," starting with a sore throat then getting down into her chest, making her cough and leading to bronchitis. Not long after the coughing started she would lose her voice. Then she would be unable to work. In fact, it was the bronchitis, the coughing, the lack of sleep and the inability to work that usually drove her to the doctor.

I saw her after she had persistent symptoms even though she had followed her prescribed treatment. Although she was very frustrated about the persistence of her sinus infection, she was becoming increasingly concerned about the fact the she was, as she put it, "living on antibiotics." CT scan evaluation of her sinuses confirmed sinus disease. Because she was afraid of losing her job (she had lost her two previous jobs because of missing too much time due to illness) she was reluctant to proceed with surgery. In addition to her current sinus medications, I started her on a regimen of hypertonic saline irrigation.

Even though she was in an "I will try anything" mode, she was skeptical about nasal irrigation. She made it clear to me that she didn't like putting anything in her nose. After an explanation of the technique she agreed to try it.

At follow up, she was overwhelmed with how well it had worked. For the first time she was "clear!" She was able to breathe through her nose. The drainage had stopped for the first time in a long time. The headaches were gone and she was resting better. Her voice was back to normal and her throat didn't feel irritated all the time.

On long-term follow up, she still hasn't scheduled that sinus surgery. Oh, she still gets sinus infections; they just don't control her life any more. The mild symptoms she now has are manageable. It doesn't get "down into her chest." Her sinus infection and colds are much less frequent. And when she does get one, it does not last nearly as long. She is not missing nearly as much work.

Kelvin Walls, M.D.
Otolaryngologist (Ears, Nose, Throat—Head and Neck Surgeon)
Lees Summit, Missouri

Special Section: Let's Hear From The Experts

Worth Waiting For

My introduction to the idea of nasal irrigation came many years ago when patients started telling me about the "neti pot" — an ancient ceramic device that holds a saline solution and has a spout that is inserted into each nostril and tipped up to pour the liquid into the nose and out the mouth or other nostril. I looked into this method and even bought a neti pot for my own use. I found the cleansing outcome very helpful, but the process seemed awkward and difficult to master. Then a few years ago I heard about the Nasopure product. The concept of nasal irrigation to cleanse the nasal passages is the same, but the actual process of irrigation using this device is so much simpler than the neti pot.

I have many patients who have found benefit from this system. Anyone with recurrent sinus problems, allergy symptoms involving the nose and throat, recurrent ear or Eustachian tube issues benefits from daily nasal irrigation with a mild saline solution.

One recent example is Teri, a 40-year old woman with recurrent sinus infections repeatedly treated with antibiotics. Once she began regular saline nasal irrigations, she noticed immediate improvement. She has needed no antibiotics now for several years! She and I are very grateful for this most useful, health-saving technique!

Julia, another middle-aged woman, was plagued every spring and summer with seasonal allergies. She experienced sneezing, coughing, itchy eyes and runny nose. Her tolerance for oral allergy medications was not good — they all made her sleepy. Once she started saline irrigations regularly, her allergy symptoms abated almost completely. She, too, is a believer in the very beneficial health effects of nasal washing.

My regular recommendation now to all patients who have any chronic nasal, sinus or other upper respiratory symptoms is to use saline irrigation on a regular basis — daily for maintenance of good health, and twice a day if they are feeling more congested or beginning to get allergy symptoms or a stuffy nose. It makes so much sense to wash out the part of our body that must filter all the microscopic particles in the air we breathe every minute of every day. We wash our skin, our hair and our teeth regularly — now we can also wash our nasal passages!

Jane Murray, M.D.
Board Certified in Family Medicine and Holistic Medicine
Medical Director, Sastun Center of Integrative Health Care
Overland Park, Kansas

CHAPTER 10

When Your Defense Is Down

 The following is a compilation of my clinical experiences and the opinions of some of my colleagues. The conditions noted are not intended to be 100% inclusive of what can go wrong when our defenses are down, but rather are examples of common conditions related to the nose.

Viral Infections

The Common Cold vs. That Dreaded Flu Virus

First, a few notes regarding the differences between colds and influenza. The Centers for Disease Control and Prevention (CDC) recognizes that most folks do not really understand the difference between these two viral illnesses, yet the difference can be deadly.

Influenza, commonly called "the flu," is caused by the *influenza virus*. This is a specific respiratory virus quite different than the cold virus. The entire respiratory tract, including the nose, throat and lungs, becomes infected. The illness is severe and can be life threatening; children, the elderly and those who have underlying medical conditions are at greatest risk for complications.

Full-blown symptoms of the flu often develop almost immediately, 'I was fine before lunch, and then I suddenly felt really ill by 2 pm. It was like I was hit by a Mack truck.' Symptoms include fever, headache, extreme tiredness, dry cough, sore throat, runny or stuffy nose, and significant muscle aches. Children can also have nausea, vomiting, and diarrhea.

Both influenza and cold viruses are spread mainly through respiratory droplets — spread by coughs and sneezes from infected people. A typical sneeze can propel up to one hundred thousand droplets through the air. The droplets can survive anywhere from a few seconds up to forty-eight hours, so it is possible to be exposed by touching a surface that was sneezed on or touched by infected hands earlier in the day.

The clinical difference between the flu and a cold is this: the flu symptoms and possible complications are much worse than the common cold. The fever, body aches, extreme tiredness, and dry cough of the flu are more intense. Colds usually do not develop into pneumonia, secondary bacterial infections, or require hospitalization.

A clear distinction I see as a medical provider between a common cold and the flu is this: a person with a cold will walk normally into the clinic, complain miserably about their symptoms, but will admit that only their head and neck are affected. They may complain of a cough and tightness in their chest, but they will not be incapacitated. Someone with influenza will appear very ill, be barely able to climb onto the exam table and their entire body will be affected, every muscle feeling sore, tired, and toxic.

Comparison Between The Common Cold Virus And The Influenza Virus

	Cold	Influenza
Fever	Rare	80 Percent
Cough	Mild, Post Nasal Drip	Non-Productive
Body Aches	None to Slight	Severe, with Muscle Tenderness
Nose	Stuffy, Drippy, Sneezing	Slightly Stuffy
Chills	Uncommon	Common
Fatigue	None to Mild	Moderate to Severe
Onset	Gradual Onset, 1-3 days	Sudden Onset, 3 to 6 hours
Headache	Uncommon	Common
Appetite	Unchanged, or mild decrease	Decreased or Absent

Overall Description: A cold is often described as 'I'm fine except my head is 'not well'. The Flu is described as 'My entire body, every muscle, every bone and even my hair hurts, I am as sick as I have ever been.'

Please refer to The Center for Disease Control (CDC) website, www.cdc.gov for details on prevention and treatment options for influenza.

From The Expert

Large influenza epidemics occur almost every winter. About ⅓ of the population typically becomes infected. It is the worst of the common respiratory viruses, causing an average of about 200,000 hospitalizations and 34,000 deaths each year. Many of the hospitalizations occur in infants, a few of whom die. Children with sinus problems or frequent ear infections are almost sure to have a relapse if they develop influenza. This can be minimized or prevented with influenza shots for the whole family each October. In children, the new live, attenuated nasal influenza vaccine works even better. It is a more natural way to immunize, and lasts longer than the injectable vaccine, even into the following year. The protection is also somewhat stronger. Finally, the protection is also broader, working well when epidemic strains "drift" away from the protectiveness of injectable vaccine, a problem which happens to some extent in most years.

Michael Cooperstock, M.D., MPH
Division Chief, Pediatric Infectious Disease,
Immunology, & Rheumatology
Professor of Infectious Disease
Department of Child Health
School of Medicine, University of Missouri

" Breathing!

It felt amazing at first because I forgot what it was like to breathe through my nose. I now have less congestion and it prevents chest colds from starting. "

David C., (college student), Waco, Texas

The Common Cold

Most adults have two to four colds each year while children can have up to nine per year. Despite the name, colds are not caused by winter weather, cold temperatures or even an uncovered head or neck. Humans spread the virus, especially as we spend more time indoors, traveling during the holidays and sharing the air we breathe. Do you think it is just a coincidence that the return from holiday travels always seems to bring on colds? I believe that with age and exposure, one develops immunity to familiar viruses, but when we travel to another part of the country and share new germs, within three to seven days a new cold virus can be spreading through your home. Once someone sneezes or coughs, the viral droplets can travel several feet and land onto another's mouth, nose or hard surface just to be relocated by a human hand. Air travel is a notorious example of this.

Rhinovirus, the most frequent cause of the common cold, has more than 100 different varieties. Developing immunity to one type does nothing to keep the others from attacking and ruining your week.

Two studies found that nose washing can take a lot of the misery out of the common cold. Consistently, over 20 years, I have confirmed this to be true in my patients.

In the fall of 1998, Dr. Ravizza of Pennsylvania State University presented his findings to the 50th Scientific Assembly of the American Academy of Family Physicians. [9] In this study, 294 college students were divided into three subgroups. One subgroup performed daily nasal irrigation, one took a daily placebo pill, and the third group was left untreated. All participants were asked to keep a cold symptoms diary. The study found that students who used the daily saline rinse experienced a significant reduction in the number of colds contracted compared with non-users. On average, those engaging in nasal irrigation had fewer colds over the study period, compared with the placebo or untreated groups.

A study published in the January, 2008 issue of *Archives of Otolaryngology* found that a saline nasal wash solution improves nasal symptoms and may help prevent the recurrence of respiratory infections when used by children with the common cold. [10] The researchers studied the cold and flu symptoms, consumption of medication, complications, missed school days as well as the number of illness days during follow up visits. The patients in the saline group showed significantly lower scores in sore throat, cough, nasal obstruction, and secretion. By the third follow up visit, significantly fewer children in the saline group were using fever reducing medications (9% vs. 33%), nasal decongestants (5% vs. 47%), mucolytics (10% vs. 37%), and systemic antibiotics and antiviral medications (6% vs. 21%). During the same period children in the saline group also reported significantly fewer illness days (31% vs.75%), school absences (17% vs. 35%), and complications (8% vs. 32%). The nasal wash was well tolerated.

This study was released as other researchers were reporting that non-prescription cough medicines do not help children with colds and might even cause harm. Another study suggested that these cold medications don't help adults much, either.

In my experience with patients there isn't much mystery. Colds, typically lasting seven to ten days, are spread by cough or sneeze air droplets which are then inhaled by someone sharing the same air. Saline washes work by removing inflammatory compounds and by creating a favorable environment for cilia to sweep away mucus and viral particles.

Everyone has some advice on treating a cold, so I want to share mine. There are three key supportive measures, which can help you while avoiding secondary bacterial infections.

- **STAY HYDRATED:** Maintain adequate fluids, both inside and out. A guide for what is adequate for your internal needs is the number of times you need to empty your bladder — it should be at least four times each day. Appropriate fluid sources include soups, water, and fruits, but not caffeine.
- **STAY MOISTENED:** To keep the mucus loose, take long warm baths or showers often and maintain the humidity in the air you breathe. Wash the nasal cavity clean of infected mucus.
- **STAY WARM AND RESTED:** Sleep often, sleep well.

" *Keep The System Clean*

In my opinion, preventing colds - and a variety of other sicknesses as well — is as simple as good hygiene. We all know that washing our hands is important, but I noticed a big difference when I took the next step: washing my nose. We breathe in thousands of gallons of air every day, along with dirt, irritating chemicals, germs, viruses, and whatever else the air bears. Once I got in the habit of rinsing my nose out with warm saline once a day and saw all the icky stuff that rinsing brought out, I hated to miss even a single day. "

Nick Kasoff, Radio DJ, St. Louis, Missouri

From The Expert

Day care can provide developmentally important experiences for preschoolers while allowing parents to pursue careers. It also exposes youngsters to a great many infections. The larger the center, the greater the risk. Once the daycare group increases beyond more than about six children, the risk of infections increases dramatically. Children in large day care centers have more infections of almost every kind, and require antibiotics more often for bacterial infections that are more likely to be resistant to antimicrobials.

Michael Cooperstock, M.D., MPH
Division Chief, Pediatric Infectious Disease,
Immunology, & Rheumatology
Professor of Infectious Disease
Department of Child Health
School of Medicine, University of Missouri

Reminders When You Have A Cold:

- Start self-care measures at the very first hint of a cold's onset.
- Don't rub your eyes.
- Cold viruses love eyes and noses but rarely leap mouth to mouth.
- Keep the mucus flowing out.
- Stay hydrated.
- Skip antihistamines, which can dry nasal membranes and slow the mucus flow.
- Decongestants can help ease stuffiness because they shrink swollen tissue inside the noses. But remember, nasal decongestant sprays can worsen congestion if used for more than two or three days (see Chapter 3).
- Humidity helps reduce congestion.
- Soups (yes, chicken soup) and most warm fluids are helpful. The warmth helps loosen the mucus; the nutrients are good for you.
- Be patient…whether you treat the cold at home, or go to the doctor, a typical cold will still last about seven to ten days.
- Most treatments address only the cold symptoms, not the underlying infection.
- Avoid Eskimo kisses and other intimate contact with those you love.

"" Avoiding The Common Cold

While on a trip in November, I noticed stuffiness and some post nasal drainage beginning, and with just one washing that disappeared. Since December, coming in contact with so many people who have the flu, sinus infections, and chest congestion, I've been washing daily, even as a preventive after I've been out in public. At home, during the winter, along with using a humidifier, I think nose washing is keeping my nasal passages from being too dry. Usually between January and April I get a really bad sinus infection, but so far this season, not even a cold. ""

Sally D., Springfield, Missouri

"" Heading Off Colds

Nasal washing works well for me. I use it regularly and then when I feel a cold coming on I increase the number of times each week that I use it. ""

Tom Rhodus, Denver, Colorado

"" Finally Some Action

I currently have a cold brought on by allergies. I have been washing my nose and am really starting to see the benefits. I had visited with you earlier about my ear issue, and something is moving in there - after 4 YEARS!!! I am confident that as I continue the process, I will see more results - for now it is just having my hearing return and a cessation of the ringing. I am still amazed that the solution to my problem may be so simple. ""

Eric P., San Diego, California

Special Section: Let's Hear From The Experts

Warding Off Colds

A cure for the common cold has been elusive. Vaccines do not work for colds because the viruses responsible for colds mutate frequently. Cold viruses and our immune systems constantly play hide-and-go-seek — viruses hiding by mutating, and our immune systems seeking their newer versions. The immune system can easily destroy cold viruses they were exposed to previously, but can we help our immune systems prevent the new ones?

Sufficient numbers of viruses are necessary to make us sick. Viruses have to enter the cell membrane lining the nose in order to replicate. They have to use our cell machinery to make new copies of viruses. They bud off these cells to spread to more cells as a cold develops. Washing the nose reduces the numbers of viruses to prevent their spread. Replication is kept at bay by washing away the new copies before they can invade more cells. Viral entry rate is the first step in determining how quickly they can make us sick. How quickly they enter is not well documented. Apparently, it is sufficiently slow to make nasal washing effective. Routine washing of the nose each day prevents viral build up. This keeps colds so minor as to be virtually undetectable by nasal washer advocates. Those washing their nose once or twice daily report rarely getting sick with colds any more. Those who feel a cold coming on can wash their nose more frequently and find symptoms disappear quickly.

Hand washing can reduce the transmission of cold viruses from hand to nose. These viruses spread by sneezing and nasal washing dramatically reduces sneezing. Well-mannered people cover their mouth and nose when they sneeze. Even if they do this with a handkerchief instead of their hand, this act still transfers viruses from noses or tissues to hands. Washing hands decreases this transfer to surfaces that are frequently touched, like doorknobs, phones, computer keyboards, shopping carts and other hands. However, people touch itchy noses more frequently than any objects. Thus, without a clean un-itchy nose, even washed hands remain infection spreaders. Those who care for children who are coughing and sneezing are particularly susceptible to viral transfers. The only sensible solution is for everyone to wash their nose routinely to flush out these virulent invaders. By this means, viral transfers by air and hand, are minimized.

The Center for Disease Control (CDC) currently recommends hand washing and avoiding sick people. This is good advice. However, parents of sick children and health care professionals can not avoid sick people. In our hectic world, people cannot skip work for a cold and children can not skip school for colds without creating gaps in their education. For those who are ill for other reasons, a cold can be the straw that breaks the camel's back and keeps them home. For most of us, we keep right on trucking. Personally, I find washing my nose daily means I never catch colds and for that I am very grateful

Marilyn James-Kracke, PhD
Associate Professor of Medical Pharmacology & Physiology
Department of Medical Pharmacology & Physiology
School of Medicine, University of Missouri

A Pharmacist's View Of Nasal Washing
To Treat Congestion

I work in a retail pharmacy setting serving a broad cross-section of my community's population: city dwellers, rural farming folk, young and elderly, laborers, office workers and people from several other countries around the world. As a pharmacist I have many customers approaching me about allergy problems, sinus headaches, repeated sinus infections, colds and coughs, etc; some with acute problems, others with long standing or recurring conditions.

My approach is to listen to their concerns and then to explain the pros and cons of a variety of approaches to help them deal with their particular problem. I will always include a more natural approach (for example, nose washing) for their consideration along with information *on various allergy or other medications that might be appropriate for resolving their particular respiratory health problem.*

Some customers just want the regular "Cold Remedy" or "Sinus/ Congestion Medication" and don't want to think about or consider a different approach. Others don't think they could deal with the "yuck" factor of nasal irrigation especially when they're already feeling bad. But I hope that in at least mentioning the positive aspects of nasal irrigation they will perhaps consider it again at a later stage.

Then there are those customers who have tried "everything" and wonder whether there is anything else which would help, or perhaps something more natural. Pregnant women who very rightly don't want to take any medication which would hurt their growing baby are often delighted to hear about how nasal irrigation can help them better cope with their nasal symptoms. Very often it is the young husband looking for relief for his wife who comes into the pharmacy to inquire about what could be done to help.

Mothers with younger children are often happily surprised that nasal irrigation is something that they can safely use to decrease their child's allergy symptoms, or cough and cold — naturally with little to no adverse effects. This information is especially useful for these young parents since the latest warnings from the Food and Drug Administration to avoid using over-the-counter cold and flu remedies on children under six years of age.

Once people understand the logic and simplicity of nasal irrigation they are usually keen to at least try the technique. I have feedback from customers who use nasal irrigation regularly and swear by it, saying that it has decreased their allergy symptoms, has shortened the length and severity of a cold and seems to have helped in preventing the development of some secondary upper respiratory infections and decreasing their sinus infections.

I too have used nose washing to help me with sinus or nasal problems and can vouch for the benefits of using this simple medical approach. It is very easy to prepare the nose washing solution and very easy to do the actual nose washing. The procedure is very easy on the body and works very well with respiratory medications for allergies and congestion.

Muriel Vincent, Registered Pharmacist
Columbia, Missouri

Sinus Problems And Bacterial Infections

Chronic Sinusitis

- Chronic sinusitis is one of the most commonly diagnosed chronic illnesses in the United States, affecting forty to fifty million Americans each year.

- Chronic sinusitis begins with an inflammation of the mucous membranes in your sinuses. This inflammation causes fluid buildup, eventually plugging the sinus cavity and preventing normal mucus drainage.

- Chronic sinusitis can be a miserable condition that significantly impairs your quality of life. If you have chronic sinusitis, you may have difficulty breathing through your nose or experience frequent headaches and tenderness in the face or aching behind the eyes. You may also have frequent yellow or greenish discharge from your nose or drainage down the back of your throat.

- Chronic sinusitis can be caused by infections of the upper respiratory tract — the nose, pharynx, sinuses and throat — but there are non-infectious triggers also. Allergies are a common cause, and anatomical problems such as a deviated nasal septum or polyps can bring on chronic sinusitis.

- Although most cases of sinusitis clear up in less than four weeks (termed "acute"), when the condition recurs or lasts longer than twelve consecutive weeks, you have developed a case of chronic sinusitis.

- Chronic sinusitis may be caused by mold or fungi in the sinuses.

- Research suggests that nasal irrigation is useful in the treatment of chronic sinusitis, with improvements in sinus-related quality of life, decreases in symptoms and decreases in medication use.

" After Years, Easy Breathing

I've suffered with chronic sinusitis for years and have tried many, many treatments with mixed results, none lasting. I have already noticed my breathing through my nose seems much easier since I began my nasal rinsing! "

Michael L. Collins, RN, Retired US Army,
Leavenworth, Kansas

" Sinus Infection-Free

I do recommend nasal washing to anyone who complains of sinus infections. I seldom suffer from one anymore. I am 100% sold on regular nasal washing. Since I started three years ago, I have not had one sinus infection. Before then I was getting one to three sinus infections a year for at least ten years. "

Jo C., Charleston, West Virginia

From The Expert

Known causes of headaches are pressure points in the nose made more intense by nasal swelling. We have relieved many severe chronic headaches simply by encouraging our patients to use buffered hypertonic nasal saline irrigation regularly. The solution pulls the excess water from the swollen membranes, thereby relieving the nasal swelling that intensifies the pressure point. This often cures the headache.

David S. Parsons, M.D., FAAP, FACS
Clinical Professor, Universities of North & South Carolina
Pediatric Otolaryngology, Charlotte Eye, Ear, Nose and Throat

" "
I Trusted My Doctor

My physician recommended nasal washing for my allergies and sinus headaches. I was reluctant at first but eventually decided to give it a try. My experience has been nothing but positive. I breathe much better and do not need to use nasal sprays half as much. Thank you! " "

Rosanne Bianchi, Springfield, Massachusetts

Special Section: Let's Hear From The Experts

Sinusitis & Nasal Lavage (Washing)

I have practiced internal medicine for many years in academic settings. Early in my career I became aware of nasal lavage (washing) solutions for patients with allergies and recurrent sinus infections. However, in those days, ways to deliver a good lavage were limited and there was little in the medical literature to verify the benefits. So, I prescribed this for a few patients but did not promote it for wide scale use. About six years ago, three changes occurred that have influenced my thinking about nasal lavage.

First of all, I personally started getting recurrent sinus infections and a worsening of my allergies (which probably contributed to the infections). Secondly, after moving to Columbia, Missouri, working at the University of Missouri Health Care, I heard about the Nasopure nasal lavage system. I contacted Dr. Solomon for more information and was able to meet with her to learn more. I was impressed with her commitment to promote nasal lavage.

I decided to start using it myself. It was easy to use but I must admit that I would try it for few days and then forget about it. However, after getting over yet another sinus infection, I was determined to use it on a regular basis and have done so (using it at least once per day) ever since. One cannot draw general scientific conclusions from one person's experience but I have found that the frequency of my infections has decreased dramatically.

Third, medical studies started to come out showing the benefits of nasal lavage. This has been gratifying because it is normally very difficult to find funding for this type of research and I laud the efforts of the investigators in this area.

To me it is clear that nasal lavage is very useful for patients with allergies or sinusitis. Lavage can lessen the need for medications. The problem is getting the patient to use lavage regularly, as my personal experience has shown.

I have found the following tips helpful:

1. *Carefully educate the patient on the benefits of nasal lavage. I frequently compare it with the importance of hand washing.*

2. *Address any concerns such as the often expressed fear that it will go into their ears.*

3. *If you use it yourself as I do, let them know that.*

4. *Tell them to keep the bottle in the shower or on the edge of the tub so that they can't miss it before bathing. This also has the advantage of allowing the solution to drain while in the shower.*

5. *On return visits, ask them how their use of saline lavage is working for them. Keep encouraging its use.*

6. *Recommend that nasal lavage be performed daily, even (or especially) on vacation. Using on long plane rides can also be very beneficial.*

In summary, I feel that every patient with allergies or recurrent sinus infections should be given the opportunity to try saline lavage. With encouragement from their care providers, they will hopefully find it of benefit and will continue to use it regularly.

Robert Hodge, M.D., FACP, FACPE, CPE
Professor of Clinical Internal Medicine
Division of General Internal Medicine
School of Medicine, University of Missouri

" *Natural Remedy*

I had begun suffering from chronic sinus infections on a regular basis and was constantly on medication in attempt to alleviate the symptoms. Not liking the idea of being medicated on a continual basis, I was open to any options available to me, except surgery. Shortly after nasal washing was introduced, my daughter mentioned it to me and I was very open to the idea of using natural ingredients to cure the infections. I immediately began feeling better and my infections disappeared. I now wash my nose daily and also immediately after doing any yard work. "

Violet B., Columbia, Missouri

Special Section: Let's Hear From The Experts

A Naturopathic Approach To Sinus Issues

When treating sinus-related conditions with a naturopathic approach, symptomatic relief is an important goal, but even more important is treatment of the actual cause. When the deeper cause is treated, symptoms subsequently clear up and the resulting relief is more effective and lasting.

Hydrotherapy, the use of different temperatures of water in a variety of applications, provides many potential benefits. These techniques can help equally in the healing of both infectious and allergic related conditions.

One simple hydrotherapy technique is nasal irrigation. Originating in many cultures historically, it is best known from the Ayurvedic tradition of ancient India. The simple process of washing out the nose can have great results both in the treatment of many common sinus related conditions as well as a preventive measure.

This technique is based on basic principles of hygiene. To perform this procedure, one mixes salt into warm purified water to make a saline solution. This solution is then used to wash out the sinuses. A traditional "neti" pot can be used, or there are a number of user friendly devices available on the market. These modernized versions often employ a squeeze bottle or syringe type device that many of my patients find easier and more convenient than the traditional "neti" pot. Any of these devices can be helpful; the most important thing is consistent use.

Another easy and effective hydrotherapy technique gives profound relief to the congestive pain and pressure of inflamed sinus passages. Application of alternating hot and cold moist compresses can offer relief to throbbing and inflamed sinus passages. It acts to pump interstitial fluids away from the area, reducing inflammation while bringing increased blood flow and increased white blood cell activity.

By combining a variety of natural approaches to relieve symptoms and assist the body's healing process while treating the underlying dysfunctions, the naturopathic approach can bring about powerful and lasting relief to many common sinus-related conditions.

Mark Green, Naturopathic Doctor
Overland Park, Kansas

Fungal Sinusitis

Fungi are infectious living organisms that are different from viral or bacterial particles. Is there a fungus among us? Yes there is! Our normal human bodies contain many fungi as part of the natural balance of microbes *(flora)* in the intestines. The interesting point to remember about fungi is that they live and coexist in a natural balance with other microorganisms that colonize our bodies. But under certain conditions, fungi overpower the balance, causing a mild infection or even a life-threatening episode.

Thousands of kinds of single-cell fungi (molds and yeasts) are found everywhere in the world. Fungal spores (the reproductive part of the organism) become airborne like pollen and some people develop allergies to fungi. When fungi cause inflammation or infection of the sinuses, it is termed *fungal sinusitis*. Despite the tens of thousands of fungal types, human illnesses are related to only a few dozen varieties.

Though infections of the nose and sinus (*rhino sinusitis*) are a common disorder, the role of fungus in chronic sinusitis remains unclear. There seem to be more questions than answers.

By far the most common type of fungus infection in the sinuses is "allergic fungal sinusitis" but the rarest and most serious is the chronic invasive sinusitis. Although this is not a true allergic reaction, it is a reaction of the immune system. Occasionally, inflammation leads to destruction of bony tissue, causing blockage of normal mucus drainage and resulting in a difficult road toward successful treatment. Re-establishment of normal sinus drainage with removal of the fungi is the first step in treatment.

Due to the long term inflammation which is often present, nasal polyps are frequently associated with this condition. These polyps then contribute to a vicious cycle of inability to keep the mucus flowing. Extended or lifelong medical and intermittent surgical management is often required. Treatment routes are still controversial but they do include surgery, steroids, antihistamines, antibiotics, anti-fungal medications, allergy immunotherapy and of course, regular irrigations.

It is clear that millions in the United States suffer from chronic sinusitis and up until a few years ago, fungal sources were thought to be the culprit in the majority of cases. However, there is a rising tide from the experts that not all chronic infections are fungal. Rather, many are related to dysfunction of cilia, overuse of antibiotics, past medication use, chronic allergies, and diabetes.

Drainage, cleaning, and irrigation are the first steps in treatment of any chronic sinusitis. In fact, if this is not done, all the drugs in the world cannot help.

" Toxic Mold

I work in a clinic in Kansas City and received a nose wash as a gift... it was wonderful. I've been using it ever since. I was told by my doctor that I have a large perforated septum as result of Toxic Mold Syndrome. Irrigating my nasal passages has been the only thing that has caused the daily bleeding, discomfort and crustiness to cease. Thank you. "

Traci Bray, Kansas City, Missouri

From The Expert

Antibiotics have long been used to treat the bacteria that cause sinus infections. Studies show that antibiotics benefit both acute and chronic sinusitis. However, the benefit in either case is surprisingly minimal and lasts only about a week at best. There are hazards of antibiotics as well. First, antibiotics promote overgrowth of antibiotic-resistant bacteria, requiring the use of more potent (and expensive) antibiotics the next time. At the same time, antibiotics also greatly suppress healthy bacteria. Each person has on the order of a billion "good" bacteria that normally populate the nose and throat. These normal bacteria almost surely keep infectious bacteria in check. It may take roughly six weeks to re-populate the area after it has been depleted by a course of antibiotics. So, at least theoretically, one approach is to simply stop using antibiotics for a period of at least six weeks. This can usually be done provided the

Allergies And Hay Fever

Allergic Rhinitis (head congestion, sneezing, tearing, and swelling of the nasal mucous membranes caused by an allergic reaction) is what most people refer to as *hay fever*. This is the fifth most common chronic illness in the United States, affecting tens of millions of Americans, resulting in dramatic costs in lost productivity and dollars spent. Hay fever causes millions of people to miss work or school each year. The total cost is in the billions each year. Doctors write some forty million prescriptions every year for allergic rhinitis; in addition, most people who do purchase non-prescription medications buy them in an attempt to relieve their symptoms.

In 2003, Pediatric Allergy and Immunology published a study that supported the use of nasal irrigation with hypertonic saline as a preventative option in seasonal allergic rhinitis-related symptoms in the pediatric patient.[11] Twenty children with seasonal allergic rhinitis to a specific weed were enrolled in the study. Ten children were randomized to receive three-times daily nasal irrigation with hypertonic saline for the entire pollen season, which had lasted six weeks. Ten control patients were to receive no nasal irrigation. A daily log based on the presence of nasal itching, nasal discharge (rhinorrhea), nasal obstruction and sneezing were tabulated for each week of the pollen season. These children used antihistamines as needed and recorded each dose. In patients using nasal irrigation, the daily nasal complaints decreased. This reduction was statistically significant as well as the decreased consumption of antihistamines. These effects became more evident with continued use of nasal washes.

This particular study supports the use of nasal irrigation with hypertonic saline in the pediatric patient with seasonal allergic rhinitis. The researchers reported that this approach was tolerable, inexpensive and effective.

Special Section: Let's Hear From The Experts

Allergies & The Nose

When talking about allergies, regardless of the situation, it is repeated exposure that causes sensitivity. It doesn't matter if you are talking about bee stings or Brussels sprouts — if an allergic-prone individual is exposed to an antigen enough times, they are going to reach their threshold and manifest symptoms — whatever those symptoms may be.

An example that I often use in talking with patients is that of a glass half full of liquid — in a non-allergic individual, you can pour in anything—pollen, dust mites, peanuts, etc. — and the cup will remain half full. In an allergic individual, however, when allergens start pouring in, the liquid level rises and at some point will overflow and the patient will show symptoms. Thus, much of the advice I give patients centers on how to keep their particular cup from overflowing, by controlling the things that they realistically can.

We can't control what the pollen count is going to be outside but we certainly can exercise control over our home's interior environment by keeping the windows shut and cleaning the home thoroughly and regularly. After being outside we can wash our noses, thus dislodging the pollen and mold that may have landed on the nasal mucosa, and preventing the allergic cascade from starting. We can use good judgment in what we eat — limiting processed foods with artificial flavors, colors, chemicals, etc. and filling ourselves with as much real food as possible. Regular exercise and stress reduction also play important roles in the immune system's function and good health.

When most people contemplate their nose, they generally don't think of it as being the part of their lungs/respiratory system that they can see. The nose is, in fact, the beginning of the respiratory system, and its health is crucial to having a healthy operating respiratory system. That is why it is especially important for asthmatics to keep their noses in good operating condition, because if the nose is inflamed, it will translate into lung tissue being inflamed.

The nose is the first line of defense for the lungs against the outside world — whether it is pollen, chemicals, or viruses — and the healthier the nose is kept, the better the lungs will function.

Laurie Fowler, M.D.
Allergy & Immunology, Pediatrics
Columbia, Missouri

" A Healthy Step

Spring allergy symptoms were much better with a daily wash earlier this year, and I just recovered from my first cold in over two years. Twice daily irrigation was a huge help in relieving congestion. (To be blunt, I couldn't believe the quantity of gunk that came out with irrigation, and that was after the traditional "dry" blow stopped yielding.)

Here's another way to say it: In almost a year of use, I have not gone to bed once with a clogged nose. The positive impact on sleep quality is hard to overstate. Besides taking up running, nasal washing is the best personal health step I've taken this year. "

James Barkley, Sartell, Minnesota

Special Section: Let's Hear From The Experts

Saline Irrigation And Allergic Rhinitis

Allergic rhinitis is a prevalent, expensive and often frustrating condition with major impact on the quality of life and daily functioning of those who suffer. A significant proportion of allergic rhinitis patients develop complications such as asthma, chronic or recurrent sinusitis and nasal polyposis (multiple polyps). While the underlying bodily changes of acute allergic inflammation mediated by certain antibodies is well understood, physicians are not sure how the treatments really change the outcome. There is increasing evidence that nasal saline irrigation may play a beneficial role in additional or supportive management of allergies of the nose and sinuses.

Allergic patients may suffer seasonally, perennially, or both, depending on their sensitization patterns. There are three distinct pollen seasons in North America — tree, grass, and weed. Year round airborne allergens (particles which cause troublesome reactions) include dust mites, pet dander and certain mold spores. A person cannot develop an allergic response to a particular irritant without being exposed at least once, and then exposed again to that same irritant. This explains why infants cannot be allergic to pollen in their first year or season of life. An allergic response occurs when specific antibodies trigger a sequence of chemical reactions which affect blood vessels, nerves and glands to produce the classic symptoms of sneezing, itchy watery eyes and nose, and congestion.

The highest percentage of people with allergies are kids; 40%, compared with 20% of adults. Treating allergies is expensive. The most recent estimates of the overall costs for allergic rhinitis exceed ten billion dollars per year, making it one of the most expensive chronic illnesses of American patients. However, those figures could be much lower than the actual costs. Despite the discomfort of the disease, fewer than 15% of allergy sufferers seek specific treatment from healthcare providers, often preferring non-prescription and self-administered therapies.

The conventional management of allergies includes educating patients about controlling their environment, drug therapy to prevent and/or relieve symptoms and allergy shots for severe cases. However these standard approaches are not as effective as doctors or patients would like. Avoiding exposure to allergens (controlling one's environment) is quite difficult for patients who experience allergy-related symptoms several months of the year. In addition, almost all medications merely treat symptoms and do not provide long-term reduction of the underlying disease. And although allergy shots may slow the progression of symptoms, a regimen of shots requires a significant time commitment, is initially expensive and demands close observation for possible reactions. Obviously, it is important to find better ways to treat the many people who suffer from nasal/sinus allergies.

The benefit of saline nasal irrigation as an additional therapy for various sinus disorders is well-described in the medical literature. The procedure flushes the nasal cavity, which promotes the evacuation of allergen and irritant-containing mucus secretions. A recent Cochrane collaborative report identified eight trials in patients with chronic rhino sinusitis, comparing nasal irrigation and other active therapies or placebo. The authors concluded that this procedure is valuable as supportive therapy in many sinus patients, regardless of the underlying cause of the inflammation.

There are several randomized, controlled trials of saline irrigation in seasonal or perennial allergic rhinitis. One of the largest is a study of 40 grass-allergic Italian children, half of whom received nasal rinsing three times a day during a seven week pollen season. Compared to children not using irrigation, the treated patients had lower symptom scores and markedly reduced intake of oral antihistamines. Thus, saline irrigation appears effective, safe and well tolerated even in children with long term symptoms from allergic rhinitis.

Specific mechanisms underlying beneficial effects of nasal lavage are not completely understood. Several factors affect the underlying disease process, which explains why nasal washing works. First, there is obviously a direct cleansing effect of the saline as it flushes out irritants and removes obstructive mucoid secretions. Second, studies have shown that washing actually removes the cells which cause nasal and sinus problems. Third, washing with saline solution improves the cilia-beating mechanism in the nasal system.

In conclusion, allergic rhinitis is a common debilitating and often under-treated disorder with major impact on health costs and quality of life. There are significant drawbacks associated with all existing *therapies, leaving room for complementary approaches. Nasal saline irrigation has been shown to be effective in reducing symptoms and medication usage; is safe and well tolerated even in young children, and is relatively inexpensive, especially compared to prescription treatment. This technique should be considered for many allergic rhinitis patients and further study is warranted to determine if nasal irrigation can prevent chronic illness from sinusitis, nasal polyps and possibly asthma.*

Mark Vandewalker, M.D., FAAAAI
Asthma And Allergy Consultants
Columbia, Missouri

" *Avoiding The Prescriptions*

I am an allergy sufferer in California. I love where I live, but I do suffer from allergies to everything in this county except redwoods and eucalyptus. I wash my nose after I work in my yard or when the wind blows grass and pollen around so much that I can't avoid it. This past weekend I went to a party that was so much fun I forgot my allergies. The party was held in a converted greenhouse in the middle of a field and it was a windy day. We played games and in one of the games, I was challenged to put two marigolds up my nose and cry out, 'USA! USA!' In the spirit of the moment, I performed this act and everyone laughed. I never thought about marigolds up my nose along with dust, grass, pollen, chicken manure particles and goat hairs.

I remembered my allergies the next day when I had such sinus congestion that I could hardly breathe out of my right nostril. I felt horrible. I started rinsing with saline solution immediately and did it several times that day. I was pretty certain that I would have a sinus infection because that is what always happens when I get this congested, but I was willing to try rinsing aggressively first because I hate taking medications.

This morning I could breathe, and although I am still getting dark discharge out with the help of nasal rinsing, I think I am going to avoid antibiotics after all! "

Cynthia W., Willits, California

146

" " *Wash Those Allergies Out*

Here in Sonoma County, California wine country we have a signifi-cant problem with allergies. It rarely freezes in our area so allergies can often be a year round problem. If it's not pollen, it's the vineyards, or the dust, or the mold we get from living so close to the foggy Pacific coast.

Many of my family practice patients are true allergy sufferers but would like to avoid using daily medication to manage their symptoms. Prevention is always preferable to treatment! I too am an allergy sufferer, and several years ago was taught nasal rinsing by my own ENT specialist after having surgery on my sinuses. Since that time I have been teaching the nasal wash technique and encouraging my patients to adopt this as part of their daily hygiene.

Once patients feel the benefits of a clear nose, they are only too willing to continue treating their sinus and allergy symptoms using this very natural method. " "

Stacey M. Kerr, M.D., Santa Rosa, California

Sore Throats: 'My Throat Is Killing Me'

We have all experienced that troublesome tickle in the throat, a burning or scratching sensation, or the sore throat associated with infections of strep or mono (*mononucleosis*). Sore throats can be due to many things. Causes include viruses (common cold, mononucleosis), bacteria (*Streptococcus pharyngitis*), smoking, breathing polluted air, drinking alcohol, allergies and sinus drainage, just to mention a few.

The most common cause of a mild tickle or scratchy throat is due to annoy-ing mucus. Allergies and viruses both cause increased production of mucus. Mucus is acidic, so you can imagine that when this substance drains down the back of the throat and is allowed to sit there, it can be painful. Most often the pain is worse in the morning and improves as the day progresses. Why? The drainage drips down the throat during sleep and one awakens with a really sore throat. As we eat, drink and swallow the mucus begins to clear away from the tender membranes that line the throat, allowing the inflamed tissues to quiet down again.

Sometimes breathing through the mouth will cause a sore throat in the absence of any infection. During the months of dry winter air, some people will often wake up with a sore throat. This usually disappears after having something to drink.

In addition, stomach reflux can result in a painful throat. If the acidic contents of the stomach reflux up high enough to irritate the throat, it can cause a persistent cough and sore throat. This is more common than you might think.

Tonsillitis refers to swelling, inflammation, and infection of the tonsils. These collections or "balls of lymph tissue" live behind your tongue, one on either side of your throat. These solid tissue masses have crevices (like a dried prune) which can harbor infections as well as food debris. Tonsils often peak in size during late childhood at seven to ten years of age, and usually shrink in size after this time. Allergies or chronic sinus infections may contribute to the persistence of enlarged tonsils. This makes sense since tonsils are reactive tissues; they filter and they respond to irritants, and they enlarge when exposed to infections. The size alone does not necessarily cause pain but the presence of white cells and other components that respond to infections (*exudates*) will. Additionally, large tonsils can affect voice quality, taste and smell. One can also experience what feels like a swelling or sense of fullness in the throat. Signs of strep throat (bacterial infection) and tonsillitis (general term for infection of the tonsils) are often alike. Bacteria usually cause tonsillitis, though sometimes a virus or even an abscess (local infection of one single tonsil) may be involved.

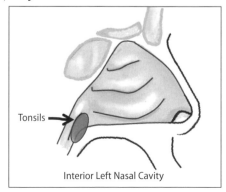

Tonsils →

Interior Left Nasal Cavity

Signs And Symptoms Of Tonsillitis Or Strep Throat:

- Sore throat, pain when swallowing
- Fever and chills
- Fatigue
- Headaches
- Vomiting (mainly in kids)
- White patches on tonsils, beefy red tonsils or tiny red dots on the soft palate
- Sore glands in neck and jaw
- Ear pain
- Decreased appetite
- Creases in the skin (elbows, stomach folds) turn red (*pastia lines*)
- Faint rash on trunk (*Scarlet Fever*)
- Strep throat is usually *not* associated with preceding sinus congestion, cold or allergy symptoms. Strep will "hit you like a ton of bricks;" one minute you are fine, the next you are feeling very ill.

The only reason to remove the tonsils is severe and/or recurrent tonsillitis, or if the airway becomes obstructed.

The Scoop On Strep

One caveat from my clinical experience is this: Parents often bring their children in for a strep test and treatment within what seems like hours of their child's initial complaint. The tests are not 100% accurate during the early stages of this illness but if tested on day two or three, these tests are much more reliable.

Often, doctors will treat the patient with antibiotics despite a negative strep test, thinking the test may be giving a false negative and they want to be on the safe side. This is an issue if we are trying to prevent antibiotic overuse, resistance, or side effects. In addition, I have found that if a viral sore throat is inappropriately treated with antibiotics, more often than not a rash develops. Then we wonder: is that rash from a virus, from a virus interacting with an antibiotic or because of an allergic reaction to the drug? The resulting unnecessary confusion can affect a child's health history and treatments for years to come.

Today, people seem to develop strep on a recurring basis. Forty years ago, if one was ill, the patient was not treated until many days into the illness. I suspect that this, although not pleasant for the patient or family, actually allowed the body to develop antibodies against the strep bacteria, so if exposed months or years later, the patient did not develop the illness. That explains, perhaps, why adults develop strep less frequently as compared to children. Conversely, if strep is treated within twenty-four hours, the body's antibodies do not have an opportunity to develop.

When you're certain it's strep, use the antibiotics! Strep is treated to prevent the spread of infection that could damage heart valves or cause other complications. But throat infections caused by most viruses (which can be extremely painful as well) are treated symptomatically: rest, fluids, warm soups and drinks, frequent gargles with warm salt water. Popsicles, hard candies or throat lozenges can be very soothing, because they increase saliva production, but should not be used in very young children because of the risk of choking.

Of course, no matter what the cause of the sore throat, medications can treat symptoms. Gargling with salt water 4-6 times per day is actually cleaning the tonsillar surface and nasal irrigation will reduce the bulk of mucus drainage, if present.

" *A Believer*

I first heard of nasal washing from a physician who said 'the simple prophylactic habit of nose douching should be routine'. I returned home from a trip to Japan about 12 days ago, three days later I came down with a severe sore throat. It was not strep. The doctor recommended Mucinex and continued practice of nasal washing. She did predict that even with this regimen the sore throat would last 6-7 days. Sure enough, the sore throat vanished on the 6th day and the virus has been defeated. So, I am a believer. Nasal washing works. "

JoAnn M., Reno, Nevada

Post-Nasal Drip

Post-nasal drip is mucus accumulation in the back of the nose and throat leading to, or giving the sensation of, mucus dripping downward from the back of the nose. One of the most common characteristics of inflammation of the inner lining of the nose (*chronic rhinitis*) is post-nasal drip. Sometimes, in my office, we call this 'Toxic Snot Syndrome'. Post-nasal drip can be caused by excessive or thick secretions or impairment in the normal clearance of mucus from the nose and throat. This annoying drip may lead to chronic sore throats, a persistent cough, or that familiar and frequent habit of clearing your throat.

Daily nose washing can relieve and, in time, eliminate the symptoms and causes of post-nasal drip.

"

For many years, upon waking up in the morning, I would cough for at least 30 minutes due to what my physician diagnosed as post-nasal drip. I learned about nasal washing 8 months ago and thought that I would give it a try. By washing my nose each evening and morning, I no longer cough! It makes my life so much better.

"

Ethel O., Pensacola, Florida

Constant Runny Nose *(Vasomotor Rhinitis)*

Vasomotor rhinitis is also known as non-allergenic rhinitis, because it often has the same nasal symptoms as allergies, but has different causes. While allergic rhinitis conditions, such as hay fever and dust allergies are the result of the immune system overreacting to environmental irritants (pollen, etc), vasomotor rhinitis is believed to be caused by oversensitive or excessive blood vessels in the nasal membranes. These blood vessels, which are controlled in turn by the autonomic nervous system, either constrict or dilate in order to regulate mucus flow and congestion. Vasomotor rhinitis is a common condition that often goes unrecognized or under-recognized. An estimated seventeen million Americans have vasomotor rhinitis.

People who suffer from vasomotor rhinitis experience an overreaction to such stimuli as changes in weather, temperature or barometric pressure. These individuals react to chemical irritants such as smoke, ozone, pollution, perfumes and aerosol sprays, psychological stress and emotional shocks, certain types of medications, alcohol, and even spicy food. So while a normal person's nose may run on a very cold day, a vasomotor rhinitis sufferer's nose may start running (or go completely dry) simply by walking into a slightly colder (or slightly warmer) room, or from eating food that is slightly warmer or cooler than room temperature. While a normal person may tolerate a certain degree of cigarette smoke, the vasomotor rhinitis sufferer may experience significant discomfort from the same level of smoke.

Vasomotor rhinitis appears to be significantly more common in women than men, leading some researchers to believe that hormones to play a role. In general, onset occurs after twenty years of age, in contrast to allergic rhinitis, which generally appears before adulthood. People suffering from vasomotor rhinitis typically experience symptoms year-round, though symptoms may be worse in the spring and fall when rapid weather changes are more common.

In my experience, the best and therefore the first treatment to relieve vaso-motor rhinitis is nasal rinsing with a buffered hypertonic solution. Rinsing helps eliminate the original irritant without the side effects of medications. Washing does no harm and is tolerated well when the patient is taught the proper technique.

Cough, Cough, Cough

In addition to a sore throat, post-nasal drip and GERD (*gastroesophageal reflux disease*, aka, excessive heartburn) can cause a chronic tickling annoying cough. Here I would like to look at another kind of persistent irritating problem, the night-time cough.

This bothersome cough can really be disrupting while trying to sleep. Often a cough gets worse at night and the reason is simple. If there is sinus congestion or nasal discharge, once you lie down the secretions drip straight down the back of the throat. This drainage can result in a cough without an irritating, scratchy or painful throat.

I often receive requests for medications to treat night-time cough, but we must realize that treating is often just hiding the source, tricking the brain to inhibit the cough reflex. This reflex actually protects our lungs. When drainage drips down the throat, the cough forces the discharge up and out into the mouth to expectorate (spit) or swallow. When the cough is suppressed with drugs, the discharge drains down into the lower airways and can infect the lungs. Using medications to suppress coughs regularly for many days or weeks can allow pneumonia to develop.

I have a guideline for my patients: Use a cough suppressant for a single night but never longer without first knowing and addressing the source. Only then may cough suppressants be used but only for another two or three days (maximum) before bed. They should not to be used during the daytime. This ensures good sleep quality, which is vital for restoration of health, yet allows the normal and natural daytime clearance of secretions.

Common causes of nighttime cough:

- Allergies
- Sinusitis
- Post nasal drip (from allergies, sinusitis)
- Asthma
- Croup (swelling caused by viral involvement of the vocal cords)
- COPD (chronic obstructive pulmonary disease)
- Congestive heart failure
- GERD – (Gastro esophageal reflux disease, or acid reflux). When the valve at the junction of the stomach and esophagus does not close properly, acidic contents from the stomach can back up into the esophagus and the throat causing coughing. This can also result in ear infections and sinus infections in children, as well as adults. This acid irritates the esophagus and can cause common heartburn, acid taste and coughing. Everyone experiences this on occasion, but if recurrent, it is called GERD.

When I was a resident physician still in training, the idea that GERD in children causes coughing was not known. But my mentors, (Dr. Barbero and Dr. Parsons) studied this and demonstrated the relationship between GERD and cough, ear issues and asthma.[12] This relationship had not been identified prior to their study. Infants and children normally have some degree of GERD which resolves as they age.

Finally, some medications actually can cause a dry cough, including some blood pressure meds, so you may want to check with your doctor or pharmacist to learn if this might be a problem for you.

From The Expert

A critical therapy for reflux is the diet: NO caffeine (caffeine is in coffee, tea, chocolate and colas), no mints, no acidic beverages, no tobacco or alcohol, and nothing to eat within 2-3 hours of lying down. We tell our patients that "decaf" means caffeine IS present. Decaf means less caffeine, not no caffeine, so all coffees contain caffeine. There are three types of tea: regular, decaf (both of which have caffeine) and herbal (no caffeine). Chocolate also comes in three major types: dark and milk (lots of caffeine) and white (no caffeine). Colas are bad for two reasons: many contain caffeine but all are carbonated. Carbonation causes belching and belching is reflux. Mints relax the valve at the top of the stomach allowing reflux to occur. If this is not successful, we ask our patients to try a low carbohydrate diet for a period of several weeks and longer if there is good success. None of these therapies cost money and they are successful in patients who will follow the diet instructions!

David S. Parsons, M.D., FAAP, FACS
Clinical Professor, Universities of North & South Carolina
Pediatric Otolaryngology, Charlotte Eye, Ear, Nose and Throat

" *Nose Washing Working Like A Charm*

I'm happy to report that nose washing is working like a charm. I coughed much less the first few days and I rarely cough at all anymore. I do it as a part of a routine like brushing my teeth. "

Barbara B., Phoenix, Arizona

Special Section: Let's Hear From The Experts

Covering Your Mouth Isn't Enough

"Cover your mouth when you cough!" is a well remembered phrase from our childhood and I catch myself wanting to use it today when someone coughs in my face. We all know about covering our mouths, about using our elbows instead of our hands to cover, about washing our hands, and about frequently using hand sanitizers. What many of us don't know about is a more effective preventive measure: nasal washing.

Sneezing is the body's way of clearing dirty and irritated noses. We cringe when someone coughs or sneezes on us. Both the influenza and cold viruses thrive in the nasal environment which has the temperature, humidity and pH they prefer. From the nose, viruses also have a better chance of invading the body's cells. Have you ever noticed how often your friends, family members and colleagues touch their noses? This is why washing hands makes sense. Well, washing the nose makes sense too. It is human nature to touch our noses on the average of three times each hour, and the chance of carrying germs to and from the nose is significant. Clearly, the nose is a primary source of contagious respiratory infections and as such should be cleansed regularly.

Hypertonic saline nasal rinses have been proven to reduce the need for allergy and cold medications, to prevent symptoms related to nasal congestion, and to thin the thick secretions that accompany colds and flu. Just as tooth brushing cleans and refreshes the mouth, nasal rinsing cleans and refreshes the nose. People who include this practice as part of their daily hygiene are getting fewer colds and other respiratory problems; they are noticing the difference in the quality of their lives. They may also be spreading fewer germs to others.

So cover your mouth when you cough, wash your hands frequently, but if you really want to do all you can to prevent colds and flu, wash your nose regularly. Your family, your friends and, most importantly, your nose will thank you for it.

Stacey M. Kerr, M.D.
Board Certified Family Physician
Santa Rosa, California

Asthma: Inflammation Of The Airways

Asthma Facts[13]

- More than 30 million Americans have been diagnosed with asthma.
- Cost of asthma in the United States is over ten billion.
- Asthma is the third-leading cause of hospitalization for children younger than 15 years of age.
- Accounts for 14 million missed days of school annually.
- Adults miss 11.8 million work days due to asthma.
- In 2002, there were 13.9 million outpatient asthma visits.
- In 2002, asthma was the cause of deaths in more than 4,000 people.

Asthma is a chronic inflammatory disease that affects your airways, the tubes that carry air in and out of your lungs. If you have asthma, the inside walls of your airways are inflamed, making the airways swollen and sensitive. They tend to react strongly to things that you are allergic to or find

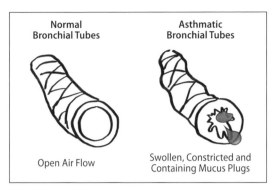

Normal Bronchial Tubes

Asthmatic Bronchial Tubes

Open Air Flow

Swollen, Constricted and Containing Mucus Plugs

irritating. When the airways react, they get narrower, they produce more mucus, and less air flows through to your lung tissue. This causes symptoms like wheezing, coughing, chest tightness and trouble breathing, which tend to be worse at night and in the early morning.

There are many triggers that can bring on asthma symptoms and lead to asthma attacks. Some of the more common asthma triggers include exercise, allergens, environmental irritants and viral infections.

Asthma Triggers

- Allergens
- Animal dander (from the skin, hair, saliva or feathers of animals)
- Dust mites
- Cockroaches
- Pollen from trees, grasses and weeds
- Mold
- Cigarette smoke
- Air pollution
- Cold air or changes in weather
- Strong odors, like those from painting or cooking
- Scented products
- Strong emotional expression (including crying or laughing hard)
- Stress
- Medications such as aspirin and beta-blockers
- Sulfites in food (dried fruit) or beverages (wine)
- Irritants or allergens that you may be exposed to at work, such as specific chemicals or dusts
- Infections

The increased costs of asthma are illustrated in a 2003 study published in *The Journal of Allergy and Clinical Immunology*.[14] This study reported the average annual cost of care for an asthma patient as $4,912 — with 65% going to direct expenses like medications, hospital admissions and nonemergency doctor visits, and the remaining 35% going to indirect costs like lost time at work. (Total yearly costs were $2,646, $4,530, and $12,813 for people who self-reported mild, moderate and severe asthma, respectively.) Families with children who have asthma report that this illness influences a range of decisions concerning home furnishings, carpets, lifestyle, household spending, holidays and pets.

Special Section: Let's Hear From The Experts

Asthma And The Nose

Asthma is a common childhood and adult ailment, one which all primary care physicians evaluate and treat.

The issue is this: like the nasal area, the bronchial tubes, which connect the upper airway to the lungs, develop congestion with swelling and increased mucus production.

For years, asthma was thought of as a separate condition from allergies. Now we know better. In fact, a majority of asthma cases are directly related to upper airway allergies. Rarely does an asthmatic patient come in complaining of tight chest or coughing without a preceding history of nasal or sinus congestion. This actually is no surprise.

If one breathes through the nose, the air is filtered and warm. If the nose is congested, mouth breathing is required but this bypasses both air filtering and air warming. Thus, unfiltered, cool air aggravates the bronchial tubes, resulting in constriction of the airway muscle, increased airway mucus production and airway "reactivity" or sensitivity.

Yes, there are many medications which treat the symptoms of asthma, and they are effective. There are steroids (inhibit the natural immune response), medications that dilate the bronchial tube muscles (prevent them from constricting) and other chemicals, which affect the immune response to "inflammatory mediators," just to name a few.

In my practice, I approach my patients with asthma as any family physician would. The difference is this: I also evaluate the nose and sinuses. Without addressing these areas, the asthma is only partially treated. In fact, when upper airways are maintained clean and free of irritants, asthma remains quiet.

The last thing I wish to offer my patient is another medication, on top of antihistamines, decongestants, bronchodilators, nasal and inhaled steroids and perhaps antibiotics. Therefore, I suggest a good nasal wash to clean the upper airway.

Over the years, I have witnessed a reduction of asthma episodes in addition to a reduced dependency on medications when nasal washing is incorporated into a daily habit. Simple and effective.

George Prica, M.D., Board Certified Family Physician
Columbia Family Medical Group
Columbia, Missouri

" A Family's Relief

I have suffered with asthma and allergies since birth and experience recurrent sinus infections. My mother showed me how to wash. Needless to say, the sinus infection cleared up quickly. I am now a devoted user. It definitely helps me deal with all the pollen. My children have started washing daily as well! "

Linda B., Memphis, Tennessee

" Free At Last

I have diseased sinuses from years of allergy attacks and recurrent sinus infections. I had gotten used to not being able to fully breathe through my nose, and gave up on using nasal sprays and various medications that only treated the symptoms.

I started washing as soon as I received my kit. It took me about three tries to get the proper angle and flow. The tissues in one of my nostrils were completely swollen, so at first, it was difficult to push the solution through. However, once I had used the system a few times, I noticed a dramatic difference in the condition of my nasal tissues. I was able to actually breathe through my nose almost immediately. Now, I wash my nose every morning and evening, just like brushing my teeth.

This has made such a difference for me that I plan to stop using adhesive strips on my nose when I go to sleep at night. I don't think I will need them anymore! The best part, in my opinion, is that this is a completely natural way to clean the sinuses and nasal membranes, which in turn keeps them healthy, eliminating the need for medications. "

Heather Ryan, Hollywood, Florida

Sleep And Breathing Problems — More Serious Than You May Think

Snoring is a common sleep disorder that can affect people at any age, although it occurs more frequently in men and people who are overweight. Snoring has a tendency to get worse as a person ages. 45% of adults snore occasionally, while 25% are habitual snorers.

Snoring occurs when the flow of air through the mouth and nose is physically obstructed, and the walls of the throat vibrate during breathing. This results in the distinctive sounds of snoring. Airflow can be obstructed by conditions which cause **narrow nasal airways**. During sleep, a person must work harder to breathe because of these partially blocked nasal passages. At times, the soft tissues at the back of the throat collapse and vibrate. Some people snore only during allergy season or when they have a sinus infection. Deformities of the nose such as a deviated septum or nasal polyps, both described later in this chapter, can also cause obstruction and sleep problems.

Nasal washing is an effective way to reduce or eliminate snoring. A college professor I met a few years ago found out just how effective washing can be:

A Good Night's Sleep For Two

Dr. Hana talked with me about the benefits of nose washing and helping me with my snoring. I tried nose washing and it works!! My wife says, "I don't hear your snoring any more, what have you done?" I told her about the addition to my daily hygiene routine. She was as amazed as I was. I can breathe easier. I think of washing my nose as similar to brushing my teeth.

Michael S. Smith, PhD
Professor of Teacher Education
Missouri Western State University
St. Joseph, Missouri

Special Section: Let's Hear From The Experts

Sleep Apnea & Snoring

Sleep apnea affects more than fifteen million people, with many patients still undiagnosed. In the past a patient snoring during sleep was considered comical. Spouses of patients with sleep apnea would complain that a partner's snoring was disrupting their sleep. The spouse could not sleep because their partner was "holding their breath." Today physicians and health care providers realize that snoring is no joke. Snoring can be a sign of a bigger problem called Obstructive Sleep Apnea. *Sleep apnea occurs when tissues in the throat relax during sleep, causing a blockage of the airway. This blockage causes the patient to stop breathing, leading to decreased oxygen levels and disruptions in the patient's sleep cycle. Hypertension, stroke, daytime sleepiness, depression, headaches, forgetfulness, fatigue, memory loss, decreased REM (deep) sleep and diabetes are a few of the proven consequences of untreated sleep apnea.*

Snoring, especially when accompanied by episodes of sleep apnea, can be cause for concern and warrants mentioning to your physician, who may send you for a sleep study to evaluate your risk.

Once sleep apnea is diagnosed, a prescription for a CPAP (continuous positive airway pressure) machine is offered as a way to increase airflow to the patient's airway. Keeping a constant respiratory rate alleviates snoring (when caused by sleep apnea) which allows for a more restful and continuous night's sleep. Patients wake feeling rested and alert.

Sinus congestion is one of the leading complaints of CPAP side effects and I have found nasal washing helps by rinsing the nasal passages, decreasing sinus congestion, and allowing air to flow more easily. Something as simple as nasal congestion can derail a patient's efforts to continue therapy. Nasal washing rinses and moisturizes the nasal passages and can help patients be more successful in their CPAP or oxygen therapy. CPAP users can improve their comfort and success rate when nasal washing is incorporated into their daily routine, indirectly decreasing the risk for stroke, hypertension, diabetes or depression. The side effects of untreated sleep apnea are very severe, and nasal washing is one of the most vital tools a respiratory therapist has to treat nasal congestion and dryness caused by CPAP therapy.

Kelly Kilgore-Bietsch
Respiratory Therapist
Columbia, Missouri

As noted above, a CPAP machine can help address snoring caused by sleep apnea, but for some people who snore CPAP may not be the answer. A sleep study is the only way to tell. I have seen many who experience snoring and poor sleep quality merely from a stuffy nose. Many CPAP users benefit from washing the nasal passages prior to sleep to ensure open nasal passages. In this situation, a regular routine of nasal washing can make the difference between restful sleep and waking up fatigued.

Vocal Cord Dysfunction

Most people have never heard of Vocal Cord Dysfunction (VCD) but as a pediatrician, I see this from time to time. It is not uncommon and certainly a diagnosis to consider when a teenager comes to see me with a complaint of coughing. VCD can be misdiagnosed as either asthma or exercise-induced bronchospasm. As a result, many individuals with VCD are treated inappropriately, unnecessarily exposing them to the potentially harmful side effects of asthma medications.

This condition is typically caused by exercise in adolescents, and by environmental irritants in adults. Of course, in a diagnosis of VCD, asthma and underlying conditions need to be ruled out: irritable larynx syndrome, acid reflux, complications from asthma medications, stress or other unknown issues.

Patients with exercise-induced VCD, particularly adolescents, learn to use breathing exercises as a warm-up before sports as a preventive measure. This can involve learning how to breathe efficiently with the focus of the breath more in the front of the mouth versus in the throat. Breathing in through the nose and blowing the air out through the front of the mouth is often accomplished more easily and effectively with regular nasal washing. Breathing exercises used in yoga practice can also assist in alleviating VCD.

Ears And Hearing Problems

The nose is a major influence in sinus and ear infections. We have all experienced the sensation of ear popping or pain when we fly or dive. In order to function properly, and without pain or pressure, the middle ear must be at the same pressure as the external ear. This equalization of pressure occurs via the Eustachian tube which leads from the middle portion of the ear to the back of the throat. When the ears pop while yawning or swallowing or flying, the Eustachian tubes are adjusting the air pressure in your middle ears. An air bubble travels upward in the tube and this is a sign that the tube is not 'glued' shut; it is open and mucus is bubbling down and out into the throat. It is vital for the Eustachian tube to remain open if equal pressure is to be maintained on both sides of the eardrum. This cannot be accomplished if there is a mucus plug or swelling blocking the tube.

Increased Pressure in Eustachian Tube When Drainage Is Blocked, Resulting In Popping, Pain, Pressure

Eustachian Tube Drainage Blocked By Mucus

Eustachian Tube Drains Into Back Of Nose & Throat

Eustachian Tube Dysfunction (ETD)

The first requirement for a properly functioning ear is to have the Eustachian tubes clear. Eustachian tube dysfunction (ETD) is the most common concern with the ear. This can occur as a result of congestion from any source, including blockage of proper drainage caused by enlarged adenoids or tonsils, or from the inflammation resulting from GERD. Even a sinus infection can cause blockage by mucus plugs blocking the Eustachian tube. The result of ETD can be decreased hearing, dizziness, ringing or even eventual infection.

Outer Ear Infection — Swimmers Ear

Swimmers ear has nothing to do with middle ear infections and nothing to do with blockage of the Eustachian tube. This is an infection of the outer ear (ear canal) and most often related to stagnant water residing in the outer ear. This is a set-up for infection in the canal because of the moist warm environment. An infection here requires a dramatic change in the level of acidity in

the outer ear to inhibit growth of the infectious colonies. Either antibiotic drops are required, or sometimes a solution can be used which will alter the pH, inhibiting bacteria from growing. This can be tried with 50/50 sterile water/vinegar or hydrogen peroxide mixture. Even a hair dryer can be used to dry out the moisture and inhibit the bacteria's ability to multiply.

Those with recurrent swimmers ear should remember to dry the outer ear canals immediately after swimming or other exposure to water. Because the outer ear does not communicate with the nose, nose washing will not have a direct effect on this type of infection.

Middle Ear Infection (Otitis Media)

I have never examined a child with an inner ear infection who did not experience a preceding stuffy or runny nose. Because of the architecture of a child's Eustachian tube, kids are more prone to ear infections. But one must differentiate an ear infection which requires antibiotics from an ear infection which does not. Many medical doctors will offer antibiotics if the eardrum appears red but we have learned that this is not always necessary, especially if your physician is able to provide close follow-up care. In my experience, a walk-in clinic or emergency room doctor will be more likely to prescribe an antibiotic than a primary physician who knows the family well.

Acute Otitis Media

2. Ear Drum Bulges Out

1. Mucus Trapped in Eustachian Tube Pressure Builds Up

According to the American Academy of Pediatrics, an infection in the middle ear (*otitis media*) does not necessarily require an antibiotic. Nasal hygiene, cleaning the opening to the Eustachian tube so that the fluid can drain, can be very helpful. Of course, if a very young child is experiencing a high fever, or if symptoms persist for an extended period, antibiotics may be required.

When only fluid but no infection is present, the condition is referred to as *serous otitis media*. The fluid often thickens into a glue-like substance if allowed to remain stagnant for weeks or months. In fact, the longer it is present the more difficult it is to encourage normal or natural draining. The glue-like mucus becomes intertwined in those tiny bones (*ossicles*) and aggressive treatment should be considered. If not, hearing loss can develop.

Ear congestion and infections can become very serious and cause permanent hearing loss, a life-changing event. This is why a basic understanding of how the nose and the ears are related is so important. But for one to experience healthy middle ears and Eustachian tubes, a clean nose is vital. Daily washing can go a long way toward relieving and preventing ear problems, including hearing loss.

Bad Breath *(Halitosis)*

We all are troubled by bad breath on occasion, but some suffer from this daily. It can be embarrassing to have this problem, despite how aggressively you brush your teeth. The foul odor can result from bacteria on the tongue, the tonsils, the adenoids or from sinus drainage or dehydration. The bacteria that contribute to bad breath are often organisms that live without oxygen (*anaerobic*). This type of bacteria breaks down and digests proteins in food we eat or in mucus and phlegm, and that process releases odorous sulfur compounds.

This is why people who suffer from infections of the sinuses, ears and throat, and from chronic postnasal drip are prone to bad breath. This explains why parents of sick and infected children often tell me, "My kid smells sick." I always believe them.

If you still have your tonsils, you may be harboring a pool of bacteria that can result in a complex of mucus and sulfur compounds which love to live in the cracks, crevices and pockets of the tonsils. They're called *tonsilloliths*, or "tonsil stones." Many times, when I have been asked by patients to "See what is stuck in my throat," this is what I find.

What To Do About Bad Breath?

- Avoid drying agents such as antihistamines.
- Stay well hydrated; drink plenty of water.
- Avoid "dry mouth," the most common initiator of bad breath and a great environment for those bacteria to generate sulfur compounds.
- Address sinus issues, including postnasal drip, with regular nasal washing.

Nose Bleeds *(Epistaxis)*

Most of us have experienced the relatively common occurrence of a nosebleed at sometime in our lives. The diagnosis is a simple one to make, usually made by the doctor looking into the nose (*direct visualization.*) If the bleeding is from the front portion (*anterior*) of the nose, by far the most common of the two types of nose bleeds, the blood drains out through the nostrils. This bleeding originates from a group of blood vessels called Kiesselbach's area.

The second type of epistaxis is caused by bleeding from the back portion of the nose (*posterior*) and is potentially more likely to require medical attention. This blood usually drains down the back of the throat. Fresh and clotted blood can also flow down into the stomach. This can irritate the stomach, resulting in nausea, vomiting, and exacerbation of the original nosebleed. Although not common, it can be serious.

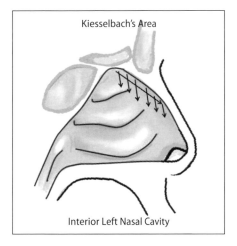

Why Do Some People Develop Nosebleeds?

The cause of nosebleeds can generally be divided into three categories: local causes, systemic causes (whole body issues), or unknown causes.

Local or common causes:

- Local trauma (including nose blowing, nose picking, sharp blow to the face)
- Drying of the nasal mucous membrane (ex: allergies, age, environmental irritation, chemical inhalants, dry air during winter months)
- Prolonged and improper use of nasal steroid sprays
- Use of oxygen via a nasal cannula, the device used to deliver extra oxygen through a plastic tube with two prongs placed in the nostrils.
- Infections: rhinitis, sinusitis, colds
- Insertion of foreign bodies, usually by children
- Perforations in the nasal septum
- Illegal drug use (cocaine or other inhaled substance)
- Surgery

Systemic or rare causes:

- Allergies
- Infections, such as AIDS
- Arteriosclerosis
- Benign or malignant tumors in the area of the nose
- Bleeding & clotting disorders (e.g., thrombocytopenia, liver disease, coagulopathies, and anticoagulant use)
- Medication side effects: aspirin, antihistamine, warfarin, ibuprofen, isotretinoin (Retin-a), desmopressin and others
- Blood abnormalities, including malignancies
- Poorly controlled high blood pressure
- Pregnancy
- Alcohol (due to dilation of blood vessels)

Treatment

The flow of blood normally stops when the blood clots, that is, when the blood forms a plug. This process takes time. Applying direct pressure by pinching the soft fleshy part of the nose can stop the flow and allow clotting to occur. Pressure should be firm and be applied for at least 10 minutes *without releasing pressure even for a second — set a timer! Don't let up even to change hands!* It is also important to keep the head in the neutral position; do not lean the head back because this makes the blood drain down the throat and can cause complications. Spit out any blood that flows into the mouth; do not swallow it. Do not pack the nose with tissues or gauze. There is no benefit to pinching the bridge of the nose.

In the past, it was routine to recommend the application of cold such as an ice pack to the forehead or sucking on an ice cube to stop bleeding from the nose. It was believed the exposure to cold would promote constriction of local blood vessels, thus slow down the bleeding. However, we now know that these practices do not have any significant effect on slowing or stopping nosebleeds.

If you have applied pressure for a full ten minutes and the nose is still bleeding, contact your physician. There are medications that can be used directly on the bleeding area if necessary. Direct chemical cautery (using silver nitrate) of any bleeding vessels or professional packing of the nose with ribbon gauze or an absorbent dressing may be necessary to stop the bleeding. Ongoing bleeding despite good nasal packing is a surgical emergency.

Saline nasal washings two to three times per day, lubricating the inside of the nose with ointment or creams like Vaseline or antibiotic ointment, and installing a humidifier in the bedroom, reduce recurrent epistaxis resulting from a dry nasal mucosa.

Nosebleeds are rarely dangerous unless the bleeding is prolonged and heavy. The elderly and those with co-existing illnesses, particularly those with illnesses and medications that affect blood clotting, should be closely monitored.

Nasal Polyps

Polyps are growths of tissue, often in response to chronic irritation or inflammation. Imagine finger-like tissue projections that can plug up the waterworks. They block passages and prevent normal drainage and normal breathing. You may have a single soft jelly-like nasal polyp or several clustered together like grapes. They are difficult to live with and even more difficult to treat.

Risk Factors Include:

- Asthma
- Chronic allergies
- Chronic sinus infections
- Sensitivity to aspirin or nonsteroidal anti-inflammatory drugs like ibuprofen
- Age - more common in people older than 40 years old
- Fungal sinusitis
- Cystic Fibrosis

Symptoms That May Indicate The Presence Of Nasal Polyps

- Mouth breathing
- A chronic runny nose
- Persistent stuffiness
- Recurrent or chronic sinus infections
- Loss or diminishment of your sense of smell
- Dull headaches
- Snoring

How Nasal Polyps Develop

Nasal polyps can develop in the mucous lining either of your nose or inside your sinus cavities. Polyps are the product of ongoing inflammation which causes the blood vessels in the lining of your nose and sinuses to become more permeable, allowing water to accumulate in the cells. Simply put, the tissue swells and over time, as gravity pulls on these waterlogged tissues, polyps develop.

To help diagnose nasal polyps, the doctor will take a detailed medical history and will examine your nose with a *nasopharyngeal scope*, a small illuminated camera that allows direct visualization. You may even get a computerized tomography (CT) scan to help determine the size and exact location of the polyps, including any polyps in your sinuses. Nasal irrigation with hypertonic buffered solution used daily will not remove the polyps but will help keep them as small and free of aggravating debris as possible, perhaps avoiding the need for surgery.

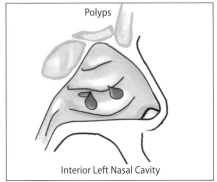

Polyps

Interior Left Nasal Cavity

Deviated Nasal Septum

The nasal septum is the wall, the midline cartilage of the nose that separates the two airways and the nostrils. A deviated septum is present when there is a shift from the midline or center position. These deviations can occur from genetics, normal growth variants or trauma (broken nose, fall, surgery).

Minor deviations are common and usually do not cause symptoms or require any treatment. If, however, the midline cartilage is deviated significantly, the opposite turbinates may swell over time to fill the resulting empty space. This swelling is referred to as *compensatory hypertrophy*, and may cause more problems than the actual deviated septum! The resulting airflow obstruction increases the risk of infections, headaches, increased allergy symptoms, and even nose bleeds.

If the deviation is minor, persistent nose washing will reduce any symptoms. If surgery is required to reconstruct and reposition the septal cartilage, one should wash prior to surgery to shrink any swelling and offer the surgeon healthy tissues to work with.

When washing with a deviated septum, always begin on the congested side first. If you are successful in having the solution exit the opposite side, then you can feel safe in flushing through the uncongested side as well. If you are not able to flush through the congested side, do not force. I repeat: DO NOT FORCE. Continue to wash gently with a hypertonic solution, multiple times, on the congested side only, until you succeed.

Check with your doctor if you are unsuccessful after a few days of trying. If the solution is forced through with too much pressure, you can damage an eardrum!

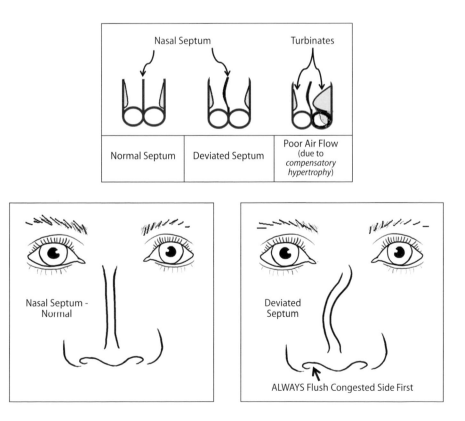

Decreased Or Absence Of Smell *(Anosmia)*

 Anosmia is an absence of the ability to smell. Anosmia can have a number of detrimental effects. Patients with sudden onset anosmia may find food less appetizing, though people born with anosmia rarely complain about this. Loss of smell can also be dangerous because it hinders the detection of gas leaks and smoke from fires. A temporary loss of smell can be caused by a stuffy nose or infection. Nasal polyps can also cause anosmia, especially in people with allergies, histories of sinusitis and those with a family history of polyps. Brain tumors can also cause anosmia so if symptoms persist, see your doctor.

Immotile Cilia

Immotile Cilia Syndrome, or *Primary Ciliary Dyskinesia* (PCD), describes an inherited condition in which the cilia fail to beat normally. This means the cilia cannot clear mucus out of the respiratory passages resulting in mucus becoming stuck and eventually blocking the airways. Mucus is an excellent breeding ground for bacteria and when it remains in place for extended periods, it may become infected. The bacteria release chemicals that can damage tissues in the area, especially in the lungs. In addition, the body produces special cells in response to irritants referred to as *inflammatory cells*. These cells can release chemicals such as enzymes, which cause further local tissue damage.

People with Immotile Cilia Syndrome suffer frequent infections of the lungs, ears, throat and sinuses. Unless treated, this may lead to permanent damage.

Nasal washing does what immotile cilia do not; it clears mucus from the nasal passages, allowing unobstructed airflow and eliminating an environment in which harmful bacterial can cause infection. Keeping the nasal airways clear helps protect the rest of the respiratory tract, especially when cilia are unable to perform their vital function.

Cystic Fibrosis

 According to data collected by the Cystic Fibrosis (CF) Foundation, about 30,000 Americans, 3,000 Canadians and 20,000 Europeans have Cystic Fibrosis. About 2,500 babies are born with CF each year in the United States. This inherited chronic disease affects the lungs and digestive system. There is involvement of the sinuses, with or without nasal polyps. The abnormal gene results in the production of unusually thick, sticky mucus that blocks the lungs, leading to life-threatening lung infections. There is also obstruction of the pancreatic ducts, which prevents natural enzymes from helping the body break down and absorb food.

Patients with CF can develop a variety of symptoms, including:

- Persistent coughing, at times with phlegm
- Wheezing or shortness of breath
- Poor growth and weight loss in spite of a good appetite
- Frequent lung infections

Living with Cystic Fibrosis often entails taking multiple medications and physical therapy. Although the first treatment plan for CF includes medications, surgery has been heavily relied upon for extensive sinus, polyps and nasal issues. Due to the high recurrence rate, repeated surgeries can be required. Nasal hypertonic saline rinses have been found to improve both sinus and lung function in patients with CF, simply by increasing airway hydration and improving mucus clearance.

Resistant Bacteria

Special Section: Let's Hear From The Experts

Fighting Resistant Sinus Infections

Millions of diverse bacteria coexist peacefully in and on our body; they perform essential nutritive and protective tasks for us. The ones that live in normal and healthy sinuses either crowd out or kill off dangerous bacteria (pathogens) such as Staphylococcus Aureus (SA). Twenty percent of the population carries pathogens without any signs of illness, but they can still unwittingly spread these bacteria to others who may be more susceptible.

Superbug (virulent) strains of SA are among our most feared bacteria; they can release grave and sometimes deadly toxins. Worrisome is the fact that SA has been able to develop a resistance against our most powerful weapon: antibiotics. This is referred to as Methicillin Resistant Staphylococcal Aureus (MRSA). Although MRSA was originally found mainly in hospitals, our communities are now becoming infected. And while there are additional bacteria which are resistant, MRSA is most well known, with the most exposure in the press.

The risk of resistance developing to SA or MRSA is greatest when treatment relies solely on antibiotics. We treat skin abscesses with antibiotics as well as opening the wound to allow drainage of the infection. This drainage is vital, much like sinus drainage when addressing infections.

When antibiotics are used to treat sinus infections, they do three things. First, they kill off pathogens (potentially harmful bacterial) sensitive to the antibiotic. Second, they also kill off the normal flora. Third, any pathogens that are resistant to the antibiotic now have a chance to overgrow and become a super-infection.

Extinction of normal flora would seriously endanger our health. Maintenance of a healthy balance of microbes is as important as destroying pathogens like SA and MRSA. Health professionals historically have been taught about the 'germs' but tend to ignore the dangers of removing the beneficial and normal balance of microbes (flora).

Too often sinus infections become chronic as each antibiotic causes yet another resistant strain to over-grow. The versatility and utility of nasal washing has been overlooked far too long. Nasal washing has the potential to lower SA and MRSA pathogens below toxic levels. The adage, "An ounce of prevention is worth a ton of cure," applies perfectly for SA and MRSA infections. Improving hygienic methods both for hospital workers and patients, protecting our normal flora by avoiding exposure to needless antibiotics, as well as draining those infected sinuses with hypertonic buffered saline nose washes will begin to address this worrisome situation.

Marilyn James-Kracke, PhD
Associate Professor of Medical Pharmacology & Physiology
Department of Medical Pharmacology & Physiology
School of Medicine, University of Missouri

CHAPTER 11

Normal Life Needs

Can't I Just Buy An Air Filter?

Air purifiers vary widely in regards to how effectively they remove air pollutants inside the home; some may improve indoor air quality. All air purifiers have some limitations so keep in mind:

- No air purifier can remove 100% of the pollutants from the air.
- The most common air purifiers are designed to remove only particles; they have no affect on odors caused by smoke gases.
- The use of ultraviolet (UV) light in air purifiers does not remove smoke from the air.

" "

Clean Air

If the air is poor and hazardous to your health and the air filter only works partially, and a mask is only a partial answer, another piece of the "protective puzzle" may be washing the body's filter.

I have really horrible allergies that I tried to ignore for many years. I'd pop an antihistamine when I absolutely had to, and just carry tissues everywhere I went. Then I started getting sinus infections that would not stay away; it seemed I was on antibiotics all the time. I was losing time at work and had no energy to do the fun stuff I liked to do on weekends. This was serious! I went to the allergist and started allergy shots. I talked to my ENT doctor and got very few answers other than another prescription. So I started looking at the air I breathe.

I put an ionizer next to my bed so the air would be filtered while I slept. I made sure I washed my sheets in really hot water so the dust mites would be destroyed. I added a huge HEPA filter to my central heating system and immediately felt the difference. My house did not feel 'toxic' to me anymore.

But this didn't fix my problems when I went outside…and I was not about to give up my outdoor fun! So I started washing my nose every single morning, every single evening, and every time I'd come back in from playing outdoors. I hike, I garden, and I ride a motorcycle. That's a lot of exposure.

The nasal washes made the difference. They allow me to leave the 'safety' of my clean home and enjoy the world outside without getting allergy attacks or infections. Since starting daily washes, I have not had to be on antibiotics once.

I'm so grateful. A house air filter and the means to keep my own personal filter clean have made all the difference in my quality of life. ”

Marie M., Sacramento, California

“ *Industrial Communities*

The community where I live is a highly industrial town with two large industries that make a lot of chemicals. At the same time, we are very rural and heavily exposed to insecticides, fertilizers, herbicides, pesticides and farm dust. Spring fever and hay fever are significant problems. Global warming is noticeably increasing the number of allergies that we deal with. Nasal washing is clearly better than saline nasal spray and lot safer than steroid nasal sprays or prescription antihistamines. ”

Joseph B., Springfield, Illinois

Professional Voices

If your voice is the most important instrument in the toolbox you use to make your living, a scratchy throat and stuffy nose isn't just annoying; it's a disaster. Postnasal drip or sinusitis can ruin your day. Singers, announcers, and TV/radio personalities need be able to sing, speak and hear at optimal levels in order to perform well.

Many voice professionals require daily use of allergy medications or nasal steroids. These medications can be expensive, come with unwanted side effects and still only treat the symptoms, not the cause. Nasal washing addresses the source of the problem and actually improves voice quality.

Singers, radio hosts and others who regularly wash their nose tell me that washing is helpful in several ways. The moisturizing effect on the vocal cords prevents drying of membranes and reduces "cracking" of the voice. Singers who wash their nose on a regular basis require less lubrication (drinks) during performances. Those who sing *acapella* especially appreciate the fact that washing opens up the middle ear canal, allowing better capability for subtle changes in tone and pitch.

Underlying asthma, sore throat and allergies may aggravate vocal problems. Stress and overuse can contribute to the development of vocal cord nodules, polyps, chronic laryngitis and hoarseness. Nasal discharge is reduced with regular washings and thus breathing is improved. When a singer or speaker can inhale through the nose without difficulty, the soft palate lifts, creating more space and improving voice quality. Washing may not be the final word in voice health but it is a very important step.

" A Singer Sounds Off

As an actor and singer, my body and my voice are also my instrument. Just as I would care for a clarinet or violin, I care for my body and voice on a daily basis. Nose washing regularly allows me to make a daily habit of clearing my sinuses and nasal passages, reducing the frequency of sinus infections, obliterating post-nasal drip, and leaving my head and nose feeling clean, clear, and free of pressure. I rinse my nose every day in the shower, eliminating any mess or cleanup, and I keep a container of the saline mix by my sink for easy access. My daily ritual reminds me that I can stay healthy and be ready for the day despite the allergens, pathogens, and other 'junk' that hit me all day. "

Ryan McNeil, Columbia, Missouri

" Good News

I am a morning news anchor for a local television station in Kansas City, Missouri. Not only do I have to deal with early morning hours and an old musty studio, but I also have allergies, which can be disastrous when trying to deliver the news.

I had Dr. Hana on as an interview guest and we talked about nasal irrigation and Nasopure. She gave me a bottle and told me to give it a try. Within three days, the puffiness in my eyes went down, my allergies subsided and the actual quality of my voice improved! My voice didn't crack and the tone of my voice actually got a bit deeper and much less nasal! I can certainly tell if I haven't used nasal irrigation for a couple of days based on my on-air voice performance. **" "**

Laura Thornquist
Fox Morning News Anchor
Kansas City, Missouri

" " *Singing Is Easy*

Kindermusik teachers often work with 120 young children a week, and colds are a big problem for teachers....especially singing teachers! Mine last too long and tend to settle in the chest and stay there with mucus discharge and coughing for several weeks. My husband and I really love the nasal washing system. We have both noticed much clearer nasal passages and when we get any hint of a pre-cold feeling, we use nasal washing and we have not developed any colds this season. We sing a lot during the holidays, so this was a real boon to feel well throughout. We have not had a cold this winter season, and the clear feeling in the nostrils is great when we sing. We are both vocal/choral musicians. **" "**

Virginia Colla, Modesto, California

 Military

" " *American Soldiers In Iraq Now Have Clean Noses*

I just wanted to let you know that my husband passed out the free nasal washing kits you sent to Iraq and the guys absolutely loved them. It is extremely dusty over there and my husband said they really help. **" "**

Sheila L., Summertown, Tennessee

Travelers

Already in this book I have pointed out how often people get sick after traveling by air. We put ourselves at risk by spending hours in very close quarters with more than a hundred other people, breathing re-circulated air in small spaces for hours at a time, and touching surfaces teeming with more germs than any of us want to think about.

Whether you are a traveler or work in the travel industry, nasal washing can go a long way toward keeping your body's filter clean and working properly to protect you. Washing your nose helps you stay clear of whatever illnesses passengers bring onto the plane or train, especially helpful if you wash your personal filter immediately after exposure. You may even stay healthy enough to enjoy your time off.

" Traveling

I wanted to let you know that I took my nasal wash with me to Australia and used it on the 14-hour plane ride back and forth from Los Angeles to Sydney to keep my nasal passages moist. It worked very well and I intend to do it again when I go to Thailand in February. "

Robert Hodge, M.D., FACP, FACPE, CPE
Professor of Clinical Internal Medicine
Division of General Internal Medicine
School of Medicine, University of Missouri

" Excessive Mucus

I taught my husband how to wash for his travels to India. You don't want to see the stuff that comes out of his nose at the end of a full day out and about in the streets of India! We both recently had a cold, and the nasal irrigation helped a lot in clearing our sinuses. "

Rachel A., Manhattan, New York

" Speak Up

I frequently have to travel for speaking engagements and I have a long history of upper respiratory infections and sinus problems. Several years ago I started taking hand sanitizer with me on flights and wiping

*down my chair arms and tray table before using it on my own hands.
I'd use the hand cleaner every couple of hours; it gave me something
to do and I figured it couldn't hurt to try to stay healthy. At the same
time I increased the amount of water I was drinking while traveling —
trying to stay hydrated and healthy. Those two changes made a big
difference in the number of colds I caught after traveling.*

*But I still had occasional sinus pain when the plane would descend.
The pain was like no other — like hot knives sticking into my forehead —
excruciating. So I started taking a decongestant before I'd fly.*

Then I found a convenient nasal wash. What a difference!

*Now I carry my hand cleaner, use it on my seat and tray table and
my hands, and I wash my nose as soon as I get to my hotel room.*

I haven't been sick after a trip in over three years. I feel so empowered!

Dr. Kind, San Francisco, California

Smokers

Here's another reason to quit smoking: Smoking
damages the cilia, those tiny hairs that sweep pollutants
out of the nose and lungs and protect against infections.
Smokers also lose the ability to appreciate odors and
flavors.

Smokers can give their cilia more of a fighting chance
against infection and improve their appreciation of the fragrances around
them by washing the nose every single day. Washing that is more frequent
would be better, but a daily wash should be the minimum.

Let me make this perfectly clear; nasal washing is *not* something you
should do instead of quitting smoking; it's something you should do while
you smoke, something you should do while you are quitting, and something
you should continue to do after you've quit.

What's That Smog In The Air?

 Air pollution and how it affects our health continues to be studied. We know that the monetary costs of the resulting medical conditions are in the billions of dollars. Our quality of life costs are very high as well. Air pollution has both immediate and long-term effects.

Depending on one's age, health status, and the air quality of one's environment, the effects can vary. In addition, some people are just more sensitive to pollutants than others and, as in many other situations, both the very young and the elderly tend to be more at risk. Children are especially vulnerable to the effects of air pollution and experience ill effects at lower levels of pollution as compared to adults. It is also clear that kids in highly polluted environments experience higher rates of asthma, bronchitis and earaches.

If one has asthma, lung disease, allergies, Cystic Fibrosis, nasal polyps, or heart issues, the effects are more significant. The ill effects of air pollution are directly proportionate to both time of exposure and the concentration of damaging chemicals in the air.

Short-term exposure can result in irritation to the eyes, nose and throat, chest tightness, cough, and asthma flare-ups. Additional consequences can include an increase in upper respiratory infections, bronchitis, pneumonia, headaches, nausea, allergic reactions and emphysema exacerbations. If one participates in outdoor physical activities, symptoms are more noticeable and quick to occur.

Potential effects of long-term exposure (weeks or months) to polluted air are chronic respiratory disease, lung cancer, and heart disease. There are also harmful effects to the brain, nerves, liver, or kidneys and even negative effects on the immune system. Increased hospital admissions and premature deaths have been linked to prolonged exposure to pollution.

Although we are usually unable to see the pollution in the air we breathe, we can often smell it. But we get used to the smell of the air in our home communities so we can not always know when we are at risk. Air pollution contains gases, droplets and particles and can be identified in both city and country air. Dust and smoke from transportation, construction and manufacturing all contribute to air pollution.

Another major contributor to air pollution is ground level ozone. This is created from engine and fuel gases and is at its worst on sunny, still and warm days. Do not confuse the harmful ground-level ozone with the protective ozone miles above the earth's surface which actually shields us from the sun's harmful radiation.

The government's Environmental Protection Agency (EPA) monitors and reports air quality in the United States. The EPA suggests measures you can take to protect your family on days when pollution is high:

- Stay indoors if possible.
- If you must go outside, limit outside activity to the early morning hours or wait until after sunset.
- Don't exercise or exert yourself outdoors. Exercise indoors.
- Wear masks.

This doesn't sound like too much fun and most likely you will still be going outside on days of high pollution. This makes it all the more important for you to keep your personal air filter in good working order. I suggest following these EPA guidelines and, upon returning from the polluted outdoors, wash your nose clean.

From The Expert

One of the nose's major tasks is to filter the air before it enters the lungs. Dust, smoke, dander, microorganisms and pollen contaminate the air at times and the small particles are caught by the mucus of the nose. Many of these are quite irritating to the nose. The nose normally protects itself with a mucus blanket that is moved by microscopic hair-tipped cells to the back of the nose where it is swallowed and the stomach juices are fairly effective in destroying these agents. When the nose is inflamed, it is not able to remove the noxious agents. Inflammation worsens the longer these agents remain in the nose.

Nasal irrigation with saline is effective in removing these noxious agents. Nasal saline solutions are available to spray as a mist which moisturizes the nose, but I believe that large volume irrigation is required to remove the harmful agents from the nose.

Jerry Templer, M.D., Professor Emeritus
Department of Otolaryngology-Head & Neck Surgery
School of Medicine, University of Missouri

Living & Working In Polluted Environments

 Many of the people who work in polluted environments earn their living in places we think of as the great outdoors. But that outdoor air isn't always clean and fresh. This is a fact that farmers, ranchers, construction workers, painters, and woodworkers know all too well.

People in many areas of construction are subjected to a high volume of airborne pollutants, including chemicals in airborne droplets or fumes, various forms of dust, particles from building materials, fiberglass, etc. At some job sites workers wear filter masks, but those masks don't catch everything and they can block workers' vision. When that happens, the mask is often discarded. At the end of the day workers' noses and sinuses are filled with the gunk they've been breathing all day.

Even painters who wear expensive and sophisticated filtering masks know that the filter just can't catch all the "overspray" that is a part of painting; and nose blowing doesn't clear out everything that gets past the mask. Daily nasal washing mitigates long-term risks as well as cleaning out the buildup of the chemicals that make up paints, stains and sealants.

Transit workers and tollbooth collectors are a particularly vulnerable group. Working around automotive air pollution and collecting fares and tolls from hundreds of people every day makes these workers highly vulnerable to whatever illnesses are going around, whatever the season. The constant exposure to automotive exhaust and fumes, and the endless contact with money and the public carry significant risks. Nasal washing can reduce the number of days these workers go to work feeling lousy, or feeling so lousy that they can't go to work.

The work environment is even more challenging for firefighters, who can be surrounded by deadly smoke, fumes, and toxic burning chemicals.

Exposure to smoke is associated with increased symptoms: nose, eyes and throat irritations, coughs, bronchitis, wheezing, and asthma attacks. Few professionals would benefit more from nasal washing than those who fight fires.

" Stubborn Welder Now Nose Washer

Over the years my brother-in-law has suffered with frequent colds, sinus congestion and bronchitis. He is a welder, and although he now is in a supervisory role, the atmosphere at work is still full of irritants. This winter he has not had a cold, and my sister says he thinks the nasal washing really helps. "

Glenda K., Joplin, Missouri

" Free To Work

I have been using a saline wash for the nose, twice a day for two years. This has decreased the number of sinus infections I have had to deal with (only two so far this school year) and allowed me to continue working. I had been afraid that the mold in my school would send me into early retirement; now I should be able to finish the year. I have one bottle at home and keep a spare in my suitcase so I won't forget it when I travel. It has helped so much in keeping me healthy and off antibiotics. I have told many people including my neighbor downstairs, who works in a welding shop, a very dirty environment. "

Mary G., St Peters, Missouri

Wood Working

The concept of using pressure instead of gravity to clean up my nose just made sense to me. I owned a wood working business for 12 years and had a hell of a time with allergies. I had to take a bunch of medicine to get by and you won't believe the amount of money that I had to spend a month. The allergy medicine made me drowsy. One day I had enough. I did some research on the web, and what a surprise when I tried nose washing! My allergies are gone, I can finally breathe better. I also got rid of the drowsiness and most importantly the insane medical bill. I am happy to tell you that I'm off the allergy medication for about 5 months now and couldn't be happier. Keep up the good work!

Paco G., McAllen, Texas

Athletes & Sports Enthusiasts

By now you know that nasal cleanliness is central to good health. Especially during athletic activities it is essential to have a good supply of oxygen if your performance is going to be your best. If the nose is congested, or the airflow is obstructed, the body is not going to perform as well as it could.

Athletes need to perform at their physical peak, yet they hesitate to use medications. The first step to increase athletic performance is as simple as washing the nose, the body's air filter. Nasal washing is particularly useful for anyone encountering air pollutants during their workouts.

Nasal washing works for any athlete at any level of competition: from the weekend players at the public tennis courts, to the world-class pro at Wimbledon ... from the guys at the company softball game to professionals playing in the World Series ... from the lunchtime hoops crowd at the YMCA to the players in the NBA ... from the family reunion flag football contest to the NFL pros. A professional athlete will never fail a drug test by washing their nose, not matter how often he or she washes.

Bicycles & Motorcycles

" Active Bicyclist

I have allergies and asthma but I am a very active bicyclist. We usually ride for 40-50 miles at a clip and, of course, I am breathing in tons of allergens. I have had multitudes of sinus infections and I'm sick of it. A friend of mine was telling me about nasal washing, and I love it. I had never heard of washing my nose or sinuses! I know I will avoid ever having a sinus infection again. My plan is to use the nasal washing system at least once per day and especially after a bike ride. "

Paul Lovell, Pittsburgh, Pennsylvania

" Motorcycle Passion

I ride a Harley as often as possible — it's my therapy and my passion. I've dealt with allergies all my life, so when I bought my bike I got a full face helmet. I thought that would protect me from the pollen 'soup' I ride through here in the local countryside. But a few weeks after getting my new bike I got my first sinus infection and they didn't stop — one right after the other.

Now a sinus infection feels really icky, but not being able to ride because I was sick was just the pits.

I tried wearing a face mask to filter out particles. Talk about looking like a nerd on a Harley! The claustrophobia and the hassle factor didn't make me happy.

Finally I started to pack a travel friendly nasal wash bottle in my saddlebags. And every time we stop for a break, I head for the bathroom or the bushes and discreetly wash my nose. You would not believe the stuff that comes out...just from riding! I know it's from the road because I wash my nose clean even before I get on the bike.

I've been riding without getting a sinus infection now for over a year. I still use my full face helmet, but no mask, and sometimes when the air smells so sweet, I ride with the faceplate up just so I can enjoy the

wind and the scents of the season. I don't know what I would have done
without Nasopure. Thank you so much for giving me my passion back. ,, ,,

Martha J., Lake County, California

" " ## SCORE!

I don't like taking any sort of drug. I tend to think "by the time I take
it and it takes effect, I'll feel better anyway." Plus I really don't like the
side effects of medication. The thing that I love about nasal washing is
that it's pretty much instant relief with no side effects - except the relief!
When you're all stuffed up, it feels SO GOOD to wash it out and then
blow your nose and feel clear again. It feels like a "SCORE" when you
get a Kleenex-full after a washing! As a runner and a cyclist, it's so
valuable to be able to clear it all out when I'm a little (or a lot) stuffy so
I can still get my workouts in. Or, during allergy season, coming home
from a workout, hopping in the shower and washing out all of the gunk
from being outside so I don't have to suffer later. ,, ,,

Janna Sanders
Fitness Specialist & Employee Club Coordinator
Assurant Employee Benefits, Kansas City, Missouri

Golfers

" " ## Woman's Champion

Anybody who spends time on a golf course knows that they inhale
a considerable amount of irritants and pollutants — dirt, grit, sand,
pollen, herbicides, and fertilizer — not to mention the germs and
viruses one may encounter elsewhere. Nasal washing is the simplest,
cheapest and most effective preventive regimen I've ever tried. Just by
flushing your nose regularly you can prevent and relieve all kinds of
nose-related annoyances and stay much healthier. In fact, I haven't
gotten sick since I began using nasal washing last summer. No colds, no
flu, no sinus troubles. So, it's great for golfers, but it works just as well
for anyone who wants to keep their nose clean and their body healthy. ,, ,,

Tree/Patricia Miller, Hartsburg, Missouri
2001 Eagle Knoll Women's Club Champion

*After four sinus surgeries and the constant sensation of stuffiness,
I have achieved relief with nasal washing. I am able to walk on a golf
course and breathe through my nose.* **"**

Donald Brown, Doctor of Osteopathy
Muskegon, Michigan

Hikers, Campers & Gardeners

 Being out in nature can lift your soul, but it can also congest your nasal passages. Anyone who spends time hiking in the great outdoors has a great reason to keep his or her nasal system clear and working properly. The same thing is true for people who spend a night (or a week or even more) sleeping under the stars. Remember also, that the harder you ask your body to work during your hikes, the more important it is for you to pay attention to the body's filter.

" *Congestion Clears Quickly*

*I have found that often when I work in the yard at this time of year, I
start sneezing and get congested. When I come inside, I do a nasal rinse
and it is remarkable how the symptoms clear quickly. I was thinking
that habit of washing sinuses should be similar to that of washing your
hands. Make it part of personal hygiene.* **"**

Bob Hines, St Louis, Missouri

Scuba Divers

 Scuba divers need to equalize the pressure in their ears and sinuses, but they should not take medications immediately before diving. Nasal and/or sinus congestion can keep divers out of the water because of the pain caused by unequal ear pressure during the descent.

Some 30 years ago an expert in treatment of scuba divers, Los Angeles Ear Nose and Throat specialist Dr. Murray Grossan, was led to the ancient practice of using salt water to rinse out the nose and sinuses. Dr. Grossan, a scuba diver himself, prescribed an updated version of that time-tested health practice. His patients rinsed with warm saline solution before diving to clear out their sinuses, allowing them to breathe freely and equalize pressure with few problems while underwater.

" Healthy Habit

I start a regimen of daily use of nasal irrigation with buffered hypertonic nose washing for two weeks prior to any scuba diving trips I plan. Before I began this habit I had experienced painful dives if my nose was not absolutely clear. I cannot afford to plan a dive trip and then not be able to dive because I'm unable to equalize the pressure inside my ears when descending. So I have learned my lesson and use my nose wash to ensure that my Eustachian tubes are open, clean and working when it comes time to dive. It's simple, cheap, and easy-to-use insurance against possible cancellation of a dive.

Glad my doctor suggested this common sense approach. "

George V. Zimny,
Hartsburg, Missouri

Conclusion

The idea of washing the body's filter, the nose, made sense to me the first time I was introduced to it more than 20 years ago. I incorporated this idea into my medical practice and witnessed, over the years, thousands of children and adults' health improved because they included nasal irrigation as part of their daily routine.

We have learned that brushing teeth prevents cavities. We wash hands to prevent the spread of germs. We shampoo our hair before it gets oily, greasy, and stinky. Cleaning the nose makes just as much sense as these other daily hygiene practices.

I understand this concept of nose washing is new to many people and yet millions around the world practice this technique daily. Have we become too comfortable taking pills? Or is nasal washing just too foreign an idea? My goal is to share my knowledge and the experiences of others. I can only hope that perhaps you will consider *cleaning before treating*. Caring for your nose, just as you do all your other body parts will pay off. Take care of it and it will take care of you.

I sat in the audience of a *Complementary and Alternative Medicine* lecture presented by L. Bielory, M.D. during the 2006 American Academy of Allergy, Asthma & Immunology Conference. The original author is not known but Dr. Bielory presented this slide, which I refer to often:

2000 B.C.E.: "Here, eat this root."
1000 C.E.: "That root is heathen. Here, say this prayer."
1850 C.E.: "That prayer is superstition. Here, drink this potion."
1940 C.E.: "That potion is snake oil. Here, swallow this pill."
1985 C.E.: "That pill is ineffective. Here, take this antibiotic."
2004 C.E.: "That antibiotic is artificial. Here, eat this root."

Perhaps in 2020 C.E. we will proudly state: Medication use has dramatically decreased and is now taken with great respect. Antibiotic resistance has been eliminated through the drastic reduction in antibiotic use and abuse. Prevention is the new treatment goal for all medical providers.

My husband, who continues to practice medicine from our home office, reminds his patients, "Pills can be poison. Take them only if you have no other options to solve your problems."

Be Well, Dr. Hana
Hana R. Solomon, M.D.

References

1. Akinbami L; Schoendorf K: Trends in childhood asthma: prevalence, health care utilization, and mortality. *PEDIATRICS* Vol. 110 No. 2 August 2002, pp. 315-322.

2. Mannino D; Homa D; Akinbami L; et al: Surveillance for asthma — United States, 1980–1999. MMWR

3. Adams, P.,Hendershot, G:Current estimates from the National Health Interview Survey, 1996. Vital Health Statistics. 10(200).

4. Newacheck P; Halfon N: Prevalence, impact, and trends in childhood disability due to asthma. Archives Pediatric Adolescent Medicine. 154(3):287–93. 2000.

5. Mathews A: Waiting It Out — Antibiotics Are Unlikely to Help Sinusitis. Wall Street Journal, August 12, 2008.

6. Williamson,I;Rumsby K; Benge S;et al: Antibiotics and Topical Nasal Steroid for Treatment of Acute Maxillary Sinusitis. JAMA. 2007;298(21):2487-2496.

7. Talbot R; Herr M; Parsons D:Mucociliary Clearance and Buffered Hypertonic Saline Solution. *Laryngoscope*. 107:500-503, 1997.

8. Miller K; Siscovick D;,et al: Long-Term Exposure to Air Pollution and Incidence of Cardiovascular Events in Women. *New England Journal of Medicine,* Volume 356:447-458, February 1, 2007, Number 5.

9. Ravizza R.: Irrigation Of Nasal Passages May Help Protect Against Common Cold, 50th Scientific Assembly of the American Academy of Family Physicians, San Francisco, Sept 1998.

10. Šlapak I;.,Skoupá,J;.,et al: Efficacy of Isotonic Nasal Wash (Seawater) in the Treatment and Prevention of Rhinitis in Children. Archives Otolaryngolology Head Neck Surg. 2008;134(1):67-74.

11. Garavello W; Romagnoli M; Sordo L; et al: Hypersaline nasal irrigation in children with symptomatic seasonal allergic rhinitis: a randomized study. *Pediatric Allergy Immunology.* 2003;14:140-143.

12. Bothwell M; Parsons D; Talbot A; Barbero G; et al.: Outcome of reflux therapy on pediatric chronic sinusitis. *Otolaryngology Head Neck Surgery,* 1999;121:255-262.

13. CDC websites: http://www.cdc.gov/steps/disease_risk/#1, http://www.cdc.gov/nchs/products/pubs/pubd/hestats/asthma/asthma.htm

14. Cisternas M; Blanc P; et al: A comprehensive study of the direct and indirect costs of adult asthma. *Journal of Allergy and Clinical Immunology,* 2003, Volume 111, Issue 6, Pages 1212 – 1218.

---

15. Ray N; Baraniuk J; Thamer M; et al: Healthcare expenditures for sinusitis in 1996: contributions or asthma, rhinitis and other airway disorders. *Journal. of Allergy Clinical Immunology,* 103 (3 Pt 1): 408-514, 1999.

16. Anand A, et al: Economic burden of rhinitis in managed care: a retrospective claims data analysis. *Annals Allergy Asthma Immunology,* 2008 Jul;101(1):23-9.

17. Monto A; Ullman B: Acute respiratory illness in an American community. *Journal Of American Medical Association,* 1974;227:164-169.

18. Bothwell M; Parsons D: Pediatric Chronic Rhinosinusitis: A Step-Wise Approach to Medical and Surgical Management. *Operative Techniques in Otolaryngology - Head and Neck Surgery 12,1:34-39, 2001.*

19. Rabago D; Zgierska A; et al: Efficacy of daily hypertonic saline irrigation among patients with sinusitis: a randomized controlled trial. *Journal Family Practice 51(12): 1049-55, 2002 Dec.*

20. Georgitis J.: Nasal Hyperthermia and Simple Irrigation for Perennial Rhinitis. *Chest 106,5:1487-1491, 1994.*

21. Grossan M: Irrigation of the Child's Nose. *Clinical Pediatrics 13,3:229-231, 1974.*

22. Grossan M: The Saccharin Test of Nasal Mucociliary Function. *The Eye, Ear, Nose and Throat Monthly. 54:415-417, 1975.*

23. Manning S: Pediatric Sinusitis. *Otolaryngologic Clinics of North America. 26,4:623-637, 1993.*

24. Rachelefsky G; Slavin R; Wald E: Sinusitis: Acute, Chronic - and Manageable. *Patient Care. February 28, 1997 pp 105-117.*

25. Salvin R; Cannon R; Friedman W: Sinusitis and Bronchial Asthma. *Journal of Allergy and Clinical Immunology. 66,3:250-257, 1980.*

26. Seaton T: Hypertonic Saline for Chronic Sinusitis. *The Journal of Family Practice. 47,2:94-96.*

27. Tomooka L; Murphy C; Davidson T: Clinical Study and Literature Review of Nasal Irrigation. *The Laryngoscope. 110:1189-1192, 2000.*

28. Virant F: A Guide to Therapeutic Interventions for Rhinosinusitis in Children. *The Journal of Respiratory Diseases for Pediatricians. 4,1:8-14, 2002.*

29. Zeiger R; Schatz M: Chronic Rhinitis: A Practical Approach to Diagnosis and Treatment. *Immunology & Allergy Practice. 4, 4:26-35.*

30. Allergy and Asthma Center of Rochester, Michigan: Medical Conditions: Rhinitis and Pregnancy. *Web site Jan 2003.*

31. Shoseyov, D; Blbl H; et al: Treatment with hypertonic saline versus normal saline nasal wash of pediatric chronic sinusitis. *Journal of Allergy and Clinical Immunology 1998; 101:602-5.*

32. Heatley D; McConnell K; et al: Nasal Irrigation for the alleviation of sinonasal symptoms. *Presented at the annual Meeting of the American Academy of Otolaryngology - Head and Neck Surgery, Washington DC. 9/25/00.*

33. Rabago D; Barrett B; Maberry R: Qualitative Aspects of Nasal Irrigation Use by Patients With Chronic Sinus Disease in a Multimethod Study. *Annals of Family Medicine 4:295-301 (2006).*

34. Sharp H; Denman D;Puumala S: Treatment of Acute and Chronic Rhinosinusitis in the United States, 1999-2002. *Archives of Otolaryngology — Head & Neck Surgery 2007;133:260-265.*

35. Harvey R; Hannan S; Badia L; Scadding G: Nasal saline irrigations for the symptoms of chronic rhinosinusitis. Cochrane Database System Review. 18;(3):CD006394. 2007.

36. Papsin B: Saline Nasal irrigation. *Canadian Family Physician* 49, 168-173, 2003.

37. Gonzales R; Malone D; Maselli J; Sande M: Excessive antibiotic use for acute respiratory infections in the United States. *Clin Infect Dis.* 2001;33:757-762.

38. American Lung Association.

39. National Institute of Health.

40. Current Allergy Asthma Report. 2002 May;2(3):223-30).

41. Prevention Chronic Disease, 2005 Jan 2(1):A11.

42. National Center for Health Statistics. 1999.

43. http://www.ncbi.nlm.nih.gov/pubmed/10691585

Hana R. Solomon, M.D. graduated from the University Of Missouri School Of Medicine in 1986 and was board certified in Pediatrics in 1989. She and her husband George, a family physician, practiced medicine together in a mom and pop style clinic for 18 years.

Dr. Hana's focus on disease prevention and patient empowerment through education has always been her driving goal. She has been referenced in national publications such as *Parents*, *Good Housekeeping*, *Health*, and *Woman's World*. She frequently gives lectures to both medical and consumer audiences about preventative and natural approaches to nasal health issues.

Devoted to her community as much as her practice, Dr. Hana has served as a sexual assault forensic examination physician, a volunteer board member of Rainbow House, a community home for abused and neglected children, and as a summer camp physician.

When she is not encouraging everyone to keep their noses clean, Dr. Hana enjoys gardening, pottery and being outdoors. She has four children and lives in Columbia, Missouri with her husband and best friend of 21 years.

Contact Information

For information or permission to reproduce selections from this book, please contact Dr. Hana directly:

Hana R. Solomon, M.D.
1204 Sutton Dr.
Columbia, MO 65203
573-999-0450
drhana@nasopure.com